Go For Broke

THE NISEI WARRIORS OF WORLD WAR II WHO CONQUERED GERMANY, JAPAN AND AMERICAN BIGOTRY

To My Grandchildren Dante and Skye Lundin
1/2 White, 1/4 Black, 1/4 Korean
100% American!

Go For Broke

THE NISEI WARRIORS OF WORLD WAR II WHO
CONQUERED GERMANY, JAPAN AND AMERICAN BIGOTRY

By C. Douglas Sterner

AMERICAN LEGACY HISTORICAL PRESS
CLEARFIELD, UTAH

Go For Broke: The Nisei Warriors of World War II Who Conquered
Germany, Japan, and American Bigotry

Copyright © 2008 By C. Douglas Sterner

Library of Congress Cataloging-in-Publication Data

Sterner, C. Douglas, 1950-
Go for broke : the Nisei warriors of World War II who conquered Germany, Japan, and American bigotry / by C. Douglas Sterner.
p. cm.
Includes bibliographical references and index.
ISBN 978-0-9796896-1-1 (trade paper : alk. paper)
1. World War, 1939-1945—Japanese Americans. 2. World War, 1939-
1945—Participation, Japanese American. 3. United States. Army. Regimental Combat Team, 442nd—History. 4. World War, 1939-1945—Campaigns—Western Front. 5. World War, 1939-1945—Campaigns—Pacific
Area. 6. Japanese American soldiers—History—20th century. I. Title.

D753.8.S74 2007
940.54'1273—dc22   2007023989

Printed in the United States of America
Published by American Legacy Historical Press,
A division of American Legacy Media, Clearfield, Utah
Visit us at www.americanlegacymedia.com

American
Legacy
Historical
Press

Table Of Contents

Prologue

THE GREATEST DEGREE of courage comes out of adversity. Rising from the pain of prejudice, American citizens of Japanese heritage demonstrated their love for their country in World War II with unprecedented patriotism and valor. On June 21, 2000, more than fifty years after the end of World War II, President Clinton presented Medals of Honor to twenty-two of them. Most of these heroes hailed from the famed 442nd Regimental Combat Team that had established a historic record of military accomplishments, including the rescue of the Lost Battalion. This is their story.

Introduction

"WHEREAS the successful prosecution of the war requires every possible protection against espionage and against sabotage to nation-defence... I hereby authorize and direct the Secretary of War... to prescribe military areas in such places and of such extent as he... may determine, from which any or all persons may be excluded."

President Franklin D. Roosevelt
Executive Order No. 9066, February 19, 1942

INNOCENTLY SOUNDING ENOUGH, Executive Order No. 9066 granted military authorities the power to declare entire regions to be "military areas" and to take whatever steps were necessary to "remove" from the area any persons thought to be a sabotage or espionage threat. It was a "relocation" provision designed to move Japanese American citizens from their homes. Most lived in Hawaii and on the west coast, and were forcefully moved to controlled areas, specifically, hastily constructed camps surrounded by barbed wire, gun towers, and guards with orders to shoot anyone trying to escape.

The headlines in the San Francisco Examiner aptly interpreted the true meaning of Executive Order No. 9066 with headlines that read: "Ouster of All Japs in California Near!"

"I am an American" became the cry of thousands of citizens of Japanese origin, many of them posting signs on their homes and businesses to combat the hysteria and prejudice following the attack on Pearl Harbor. The cry went largely unheeded. From March to May 1942, more than 110,000 American citizens were uprooted from their homes and moved to "relocation camps" in Arizona, Arkansas, Idaho, California, Utah, Colorado, and Wyoming. Businesses were lost, homes sold quickly and far below market value; families were separated, privacy and dignity stripped from men, women and children, all because of their ethnic heritage. Persons with as little as one-sixth Japanese heritage. Even Japanese children raised in white foster homes were deemed "potential threats to national security." During one Congressional hearing on the matter a Japanese-American asked, "Has the Gestapo come to America?

To The Rescue

SERGEANT EDWARD GUY knew how it felt to be a prisoner, he had lived the life of confinement for the last seven days. There was no barbed wire to confine him, no gun tower to prevent his escape. Only 700 German soldiers that had built a wall of death around his unit, the 1st Battalion, 141st Regiment, 36th Infantry Division. It was October 30, 1944

A week earlier the 275-man battalion had dug in on the heavily wooded hillside in the rugged Vosges Mountains. Suddenly surrounded, they were cut off from all support, alone, and without food and water. That first night a message had been sent to regimental headquarters to report their situation. The coded message read:

"No rations, no water, no communications with headquarters... four litter cases."

Shortly after the Germans had surrounded this unit, a 36-man patrol had been dispatched early on, but only five of those men returned. The soldiers were hungry, thirsty, cold, and alone. The battalion had been whittled down to 211 men who would become known as the soldiers of the "Lost Battalion".

The men of the 36th Infantry were no strangers to heroism. Their campaign in Italy had yielded heroes the likes of Commando Kelly, Jim Logan, and William Crawford. Perhaps it was the example of men of valor such as these that had sustained the 211 survivors of the "Lost Battalion" for a full week. But time was running out as quickly as was ammunition. Sergeant Guy knew that his beleaguered soldiers needed more than courage if they were to survive... they needed a miracle.

Peering through the early morning mist from his outpost, Sergeant Guy noticed movement. He gripped his rifle firmly and strained his eyes against the fog, prepared to go down fighting. Slowly the image of a soldier approaching his position began to take shape. In the distance the man seemed quite small. Even as he continued up the hill, closer to Sergeant Guy's position, his stature grew only slightly.

The approaching soldier was close enough now for Sergeant Guy to recognize the uniform. Then he noticed the eyes, the oval eyes of oriental heritage. It was a Japanese soldier in an American uniform. A feeling of euphoria swept over the exhausted sergeant. He'd seen these soldiers before, Nisei warriors of the Japanese-American unit that lived by the motto "Go For Broke." The Lost Battalion's miracle had been delivered... all the way from Hawaii.

The "Purple Heart Battalion"

*General Marshall... gave me very strict personal instructions...
to report to him immediately the outcome in your first baptism
of fire. After your first engagement, I said, "They performed
magnificently on the field of battle. I've never had such fine
soldiers. Send me all you got."*

General Mark W. Clark

WEDNESDAY MORNING, SEPTEMBER 29, 1943, the 3d Platoon of
B Company moved slowly through the Italian countryside
near Chinsana, as they knew the enemy was nearby. Two days earlier
one of the battalion's squad leaders, Sergeant Conrad Tsukayama
had been wounded by an enemy mine. He was the first casualty of
the 100th Infantry Battalion since their arrival in North Africa on
September 2nd. Unfortunately, he would not be the last.

Initially the 1,432-man unit had been detailed the relatively safe
task of guarding supply trains in North Africa, but Colonel Turner
knew his young Nisei had come to Europe to fight. In training they
proved to be among the best, despite their slight stature (the average
Japanese-American soldier was only 5'4" tall and weighed a mere
125 pounds.) Colonel Turner was determined to allow them the
chance to prove their mettle in combat as well. The 100th arrived in
Salerno, Italy on September 19th.

Just ten days after their arrival in Italy, the 100th lead the advance
into Monte Milleto. Sergeant Shigeo "Joe" Takata's platoon was the
point element, leading the rest of the battalion along a portion of
road bordered by a gully on one side and an olive grove on the other.
The advance element had just rounded an "S" curve at 0915, when
the ground began to rumble with the sudden force of explosions.
Enemy mortars and artillery began to rain from the heavens,
driving the untested soldiers of the 100th to the ground. From a

clearing ahead of them came the sound of enemy machine guns. Sergeant Takata rose and began to advance towards the enemy gun, deliberately exposing himself to draw fire and locate the enemy position. The other young soldiers watched in horror as an enemy round struck him in the head, driving him to the ground. To their astonishment, the sergeant slowly began to rise back up, blood masking his face. He was waving... pointing... directing fire to the position of the enemy gun. The Nisei from 3rd platoon went on the offensive, moving and shooting as the wounded Sergeant directed them, until the enemy position was destroyed. Glancing back for new orders, the soldiers no longer saw their Sergeant. Slumping back to the ground, the last drops of his Nisei blood had stained the Italian soil. Takata was the 100th Infantry Battalion's first Distinguished Service Cross recipient, and they had lost their first brother.

Before the day ended, there would be a second. In the drive to Monte Milleto the 100th tasted first blood. In two days they covered seven miles and captured two towns. They proved their courage and set the stage for a legacy unmatched in military history. Along the way, during their first week of battle, they buried three of their brothers and sent 23 wounded comrades back for medical attention.

DESPITE ITALY'S SURRENDER to the Allies the day before Lieutenant General Mark Clark's Allied 5th Army landed at Salerno on September 9, 1944, the battle for Italy would be a long and bitter campaign. German Field Marshal Kesselring sent six divisions of Axis troops to fend off the invading force. When the 100th landed at Salerno ten days behind the initial invading force, the untested Nisei would face battle hardened, crack German troops.

The ultimate goal of the Allied Fifth Army was to push northwest from Salerno to Naples, then on to liberate Rome, a distance of almost 200 miles. The task would take nine months. Along the way the soldiers were forced to cross the Rapido River; fight past the monastery at Monte Cassino, make the landing at Anzio; survive a live volcano, and endure the harsh Italian winter. They would also have to do all of this in the rugged terrain of the mighty Apennine Mountain Range.

The Apennines traverse the full length of Italy, rugged and heavily forested valleys, ridges, and mountains reaching 6,000 feet. It was a textbook infantry battleground that tested the endurance, training and discipline of every platoon, battalion and regiment. The nine-month ordeal would result in two Campaign Battle Stars for the "Purple Heart Battalion" and their first Presidential Unit Citation. The awards would be purchased with Nisei blood.

Thet first week of battle was the prelude for things to come. The 100th continued north throughout the month of October, crossing the Volturno River no less than six times and driving slowly towards Naples. The Germans mounted counter-attacks in force, as well as ambushing the advancing Nisei from hidden positions in stone farm-houses, high ridges, and thick timber. Deadly German Messerchmidts

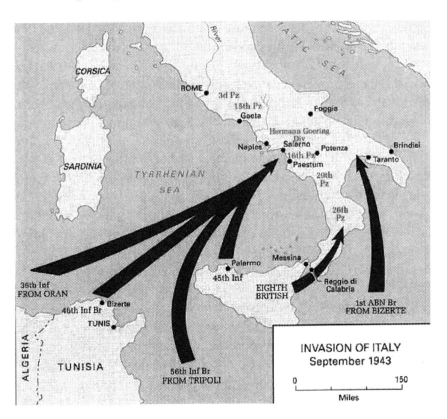

rained on the infantrymen from the skies. In one three-day October action, 21 members of the 100th were killed and 67 wounded.

More feared than the hidden snipers or Messerschmidts were the German *Nebelwerfer* rockets that rained death on the soldiers from a distance. The wheel mounted launchers held six large tubes that could propel the rockets in rapid succession, streaking with a piercing cry through the air to land among the Americans. The soldiers dubbed them "screaming mimies".

The 100th continued their move north through Benevento, crossing the winding Volturno River the first time in early-October, then doubling back to cross it a second time on October 18th. Waiting for them at a road junction near San Angelo d'Alife was Field Marshal Kesselring's crack 29th Grenadier Regiment. From October 20 to 22 the men of the 100th, along with the 3rd Battalion of the 133d Regiment fought a bitter contest with these troops. Despite the German's well-hidden and carefully reinforced machine gun positions, the constant rain of "screaming mimies," and deadly minefield, the Americans prevailed. During the battle Private Masao Awakuni became the second member of the 100th in less than 30 days to earn the Distinguished Service Cross. The battles continued, from one hill to the next, an almost daily struggle to stay alive amid enemy fire. On the last day of October, twelve more members of the "Purple Heart Battalion" were wounded when Company A and Company C were attacked by German fighter planes near Ciorlano.

Lieutenant Young Oak Kim came to the 100th Infantry Battalion during the advanced combat readiness phase at Camp Shelby, Mississippi. The 24 year-old soldier was the kind of officer every enlisted man had seen far too often, and hoped to avoid. Fresh out of OCS (Officer Candidate School) at Fort Benning, Georgia, Kim was "gung-ho." To make matters worse, he was not Japanese. Eight years earlier he had arrived in the United States as a stow-away from Korea. Kim pushed the men of the 100th, endured disdain from the enlisted men and the dislike of his fellow officers (initially most of the officers of the 100th were Caucasian), but gradually earned their respect. Upon landing with the unit in Italy, his cool leadership in combat and concern for the welfare of his troops quickly earned praised. His tenacity and courage on the battlefields won their admiration as well.

On November 3, 1943 the 100th was ordered to make their third early morning crossing of the Volturno River near Ciorlano. After the area had been pounded by a heavy midnight artillery barrage, the 100th and the second battalion of the 133d Infantry set out. At about 0400, B Company of the 100th began crossing the cold, swift waters of the Volturno. The Nisei scrambled up the far bank cold and wet and breathing with exertion, only to find themselves in a minefield. A sudden barrage of mis-placed friendly artillery, followed by an immediate response by German artillery, caught the soldiers in mid crossing. More than 30 Nisei fell to the deadly attacks that kept raining down from the skies. Stumbling up from the riverbanks, the soldiers quickly assembled to move towards their destination on Route 85, four miles away. In the darkness, confusion arose as to which direction the company should travel. The lead platoon walked into a minefield, adding seven more men to the casualty list.

Lieutenant Kim's platoon moved to the point, backtracking and then setting out in the direction Kim led until a road came into view. The fearless lieutenant moved ahead alone in the darkness to scout it. Even in the darkness it was not hard to follow the brave lieutenant who always wore a knit cap in lieu of a steel helmet. (Lieutenant Kim stated he couldn't think straight with something heavy on his head.)

Reaching the top of a stone wall, Kim stood and waved the men forward. Suddenly German bullets tore through the air and Kim fell to the ground. In the midst of the furious exchange, Staff Sergeant Robert Ozaki was enraged at the sudden death or capture of the brave lieutenant. Almost reflexively he shouted over the din of battle, "Fix Bayonets." With yells of "Banzai" the entire front line of Nisei rose and advanced on the German guns. The first bayonet charge in Italy of World War II, coupled with the tenacious "Banzai" attack, stunned the Germans. As the line broke over the wall, they found their lieutenant, alive and throwing grenades at the enemy machine gun nests.

Before the Volturno River action ended, Lieutenant Kim was

wounded yet again. He returned to fight with his men during the campaign to rescue the "Lost Battalion" a year later in France. Promoted to Captain, he earned two Purple Hearts, the Silver Star, and became the only Korean-American of World War II to be awarded the Distinguished Service Cross.

From that first taste of combat on September 29th through the first week of November, the men of the 100th Infantry Battalion saw almost daily combat as they slugged their way through the Italian mountain range. On November 6th, three forward observers from D Company earned Silver Star Medals. None of them would ever wear the award; they died in their moment of valor. Units of the 45th Division relieved a badly decimated, but valiant 100th. In their first six weeks of combat they had suffered nearly 25 percent casualties, with three officers killed in action, 75 enlisted men killed, and 239 wounded

The day before Thanksgiving, after a much-needed two-week rest, the "Purple Heart Battalion" was called back into action. Among the many battles in their quest to push the Germans out the hills was the November 28-29 battle near Cerasuolo. Staff Sergeant Allan Ohata, along with his squad leader and three men was ordered to protect the platoon's flanks. Ohata positioned his small force carefully. Suddenly, 40 enemy soldiers attacked his position with rifle and machine gun fire. Sergeant Ohata fought back furiously until he heard the rifleman to his left call for help.

Private Mikio Hasemoto had faced down two German machine gunners, firing four clips before his own gun was shot and damaged. As more enemy advanced, Sergeant Ohata rushed fifteen yards, being fully exposed to the enemy's fusillade, to shore up the position while Hasemoto dashed back to the rear to get another automatic rifle.

Together, Ohata and Hasemoto repulsed the attack, killing 20 enemy soldiers. When Hasemoto's second rifle jammed, he again

Allan Ohata

dashed through the hail of enemy fire to find a working M-1 rifle. Together the two Americans killed 37 of the enemy. As the surviving Germans attempted to flee, the intrepid soldiers attacked, killing one, wounding another, and capturing the third. Later, when a second force of 14 Germans attacked, Ohata and his fearless rifleman again stood their ground, killing four, wounding three, and causing the remaining enemy to retreat. The following day both men

Mikio Hasemoto

continued to battle the advancing enemy. They held their ground, repulsed every assault, but in the end Private Hasemoto was killed in action.

For his repeated heroic stands at Cerasuolo, Private Hasemoto was posthumously awarded the Distinguished Service Cross (DSC). Staff Sergeant Ohata also received the DSC, and continued with the 100th Infantry Battalion, eventually being promoted to Captain. Fifty-seven years later, the DSCs awarded to Hasemoto and Ohata were upgraded to Medals of Honor.

That same day, Alpha Company was making a flanking assault on a high hill held by the enemy when their unit was pinned down by grenades, rifle and machine gun fire. Private Shizuya Hayashi rose to his feet, his machine gun firing from the hip while suspended from a shoulder sling, to make a lone assault on the enemy. His courage and superb marksmanship enabled him to kill all the enemy soldiers and take the enemy position. The unit moved forward 200 yards and was pinned down a second time, this time by an enemy anti-aircraft position. Again Private Hayashi went on the offensive, knocking out the new enemy threat. Through both actions of single-handedly destroying two enemy positions, he killed 20 enemy soldiers and captured four

Shizuya Hayashi

more. Like Ohata and Hasemoto, Private Hayashi was awarded the Distinguished Service Cross (DSC). Fifty-seven years later he was the only DSC recipient of the battle at Cerasuolo to survive to wear his upgraded Medal of Honor. Staff Sergeant Ohata was unable to personally receive his upgraded award; he had died in 1977.

The blizzards of December in the high Apennine Mountain Range made fighting difficult and life unbearable. Still the 100th took hill after hill in the push towards Naples. Along the way the unit continued to suffer tremendous casualties. By January the 1,400-man battalion that had arrived in Europe just four months earlier was down to only 800 men. They were indeed, the "Purple Heart Battalion," winding up their first campaign and preparing for a second... the long awaited assault on Monte Cassino and the march into Rome. Slowly replacements were filtering in, but not fast enough to bring the battalion to strength. Back home, more Nisei were training, most of them Hawaiian boys who had adopted their own slogan: Go For Broke!

I Am An American

"Hawaii is our home; the United States our country. We know but one loyalty and that is to the Stars and Stripes. We wish to do our part as loyal Americans in every way possible and we hereby offer ourselves for whatever service you may see fit to use us."

(From a petition sent to Hawaiian Military Governor Lieutenant General Delos C. Emmons by 155 citizens of Japanese ancestry, shortly after the attack on Pearl Harbor)

IN 1941 MORE than 5,000 Japanese-Americans were serving in the United States military. Pearl Harbor changed all that. In the hysteria and paranoia that followed the attack, young Nisei (second generation Japanese Americans) were summarily discharged from the service. Even as young men of other races swamped military recruiting offices to volunteer their services in defense of their beloved country, young Japanese were quickly classified as 4-F (unfit for military service) or 4-C (enemy aliens). Despite the fact that these young Nisei were born in America, held U.S. Citizenship, and pledged their allegiance to the Stars and Stripes,

Newspaper announce the impending displacement of American's of Japanese descent.

Suffering from the backlash after the attack on Pearl Harbor a day earlier, a store owner reminds his patrons of his citizenship and not his ancestry.

their desire to serve was quickly ignored. The first battle the young men who would become the "Purple Heart Battalion" faced was not on foreign shores against an armed enemy, it was a battle at home against fear, prejudice and often outright hatred—a battle to gain the *right* to fight

Japanese Americans were hardest hit back on the Mainland. The three Pacific coast states of Washington, Oregon and California were home to 112,353 Japanese Americans. As the United States struggled in the early months after Pearl Harbor to rebuild the Pacific fleet and mount a response to the "Day of Infamy," a stunned American population often made these citizens the subjects of their desire for revenge. President Roosevelt's Executive Order 9066 led to the virtual imprisonment of many of these citizens.

The fact that mainland Japanese Americans received the worst of

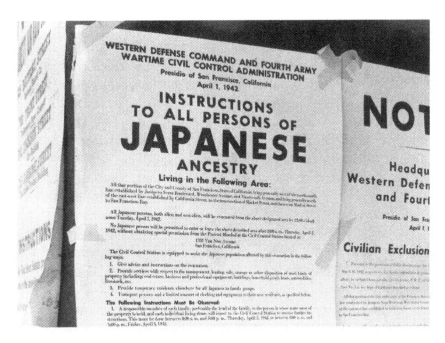

Posted Exclusion Order directing removal of persons of Japanese ancestry from areas in San Francisco. Evacuees were housed in War Relocation Authority centers for the duration of the war.

it was no indication that the situation was much better in Hawaii. In the weeks following Pearl Harbor, Hawaiian Military Governor Lieutenant General Delos C. Emmons demonstrated a reluctance to deport Hawaii's Japanese citizens. Not only did they comprise 37% of the territory's population, they were essential to its economy. Nonetheless, within weeks of the first attack from Imperial Japan, General Emmons discharged all Japanese from the Hawaiian Territorial Guard and the 298th and 299th Regiments of the National Guard of Hawaii. The young men who had the most to prove, the greatest reason to fight for their homeland, were denied the chance to serve. Only they would not be denied.

The discharged Japanese veterans appealed to General Emmons to allow them to support the war effort of their nation in any capacity. Their persistence paid off, and finally the Military

Governor consented to allow some of them opportunity to function in "support" roles. Though these "support roles" usually consisted of the most menial tasks, the young Nisei performed them with dedication and determination. General Emmons took note of their patriotism, their determination, and saw beyond the hysteria and paranoia. He recommended to the War Department that these veterans of pre-Pearl Harbor Service be formed into a special unit, shipped to the mainland, and trained for combat.

On May 26, 1942 General George C. Marshall responded, establishing the Hawaiian Provisional Battalion, returning to military service many young Nisei who had been summarily discharged after the December 7, 1941 attack. From these, 1,300 were selected to ship out on June 5th under the guidance of 29 white officers ,and commanded by Lieutenant Colonel Farrant Turner. By mid-June the unit was attached to the 2nd Army at Camp McCoy, Wisconsin and preparing for six months of basic training. The Hawaiian Provisional Battalion was redesignated the 100th Infantry Battalion. The battalion's motto: "Remember Pearl Harbor"

WHEN THE 100TH Infantry Battalion began training at Camp McCoy in June 1942 its soldiers faced prejudice, suspicion and distrust, not only from other soldiers but also from highly placed military and political leaders as well. Even as the unit's training began, the War Department announced it wouldn't "accept for service with the armed forces, Japanese or persons of Japanese extraction, regardless of citizenship status or other factors." *(June 17, 1942)* The progress of the 100th led to new dialog about the formation of a Japanese American unit, but on September 14, 1942 it was announced that the call for such a unit had been rejected "because of the universal distrust in which they (the Japanese Americans) are held."

The recruits at Camp McCoy were aware of the prejudice and mistrust, but most were not aware just how deeply felt it was in the higher echelons of the military command. Some of the all white officers and NCOs assigned to train them were schooled in psychology and were planted among them to test not only their physical and military abilities, but also their loyalty. After the war, reports surfaced of daily reports not only on the progress of the unit, but on the loyalty and suitability for service of individual soldiers, surreptitiously sent to higher echelons from clandestine mail drops.

No one could have predicted the wide-ranging impact of these ill-conceived reports. Designed to "weed out" the untrustworthy Nisei soldiers and validate resistance to an all-Japanese military unit, the patriotism and dedication of the soldiers of the 100th had the opposite effect. During the training phase, five recruits of the 100th received the Soldier's Medal for their heroism in rescuing several local civilians who almost drowned on a frozen Wisconsin lake.

On October 31, 1942 twenty-six members of Bravo Company, 100th Infantry Battalion left Camp McCoy under a "secret transfer" to Cat Island where they served for five months as "bait" in training attack dogs for use in "sniffing out" Japanese soldiers in the Pacific theater. This experiment was based upon the supposed assumption that dogs could locate enemy soldiers hidden in the caves and jungles of the Pacific, based on the Japanese' purported "unique scent." During this tenure, another member of the 100th earned a Soldier's Medal, and two received the Legion of Merit.

By the time the men of the 100th finished their basic military training in December and prepared to ship out to Camp Shelby, Mississippi for advanced training, the young Nisei had given military and political leaders more than ample reason to see the error of their earlier doubts, suspicion and prejudice. On February 1, 1943 President Roosevelt announced the formation of an all Japanese-American military unit, composed of volunteers from Hawaii and the mainland. The new unit would be designated the 442nd Regimental Combat Team, but would go down in history based upon the unit's motto: "Go For Broke"

In Honolulu, thousands of young Japanese men milled anxiously about, waiting for their names to be called. On February 1, 1943, President Roosevelt had called for the formation of a new military unit, composed entirely of volunteers of Japanese ancestry. A call for enlistees followed in hopes of meeting the quota of 3,000 Japanese-American volunteers from the mainland, and 1,500 from Hawaii. In Hawaii, more than a thousand volunteered the first day of the

Nisei recruits snap to attention shortly after arriving at Camp Shelby, Mississippi

Staff Sergeant Harry Hijimoto lectures on the proper use of hand grenades.

Combat trainees Pvt. Takeshi Omuro fires machine gun as Pvt. Kentoku Nakasone feeds the cartridge belt to the weapon.

announcement and now as they gathered for the roll call of those accepted for duty, there were nearly 10,000 volunteers.

From the microphone, a voice began to read the names of those young men selected, in alphabetical order. When the long list had been read, those selected said their *good-byes* and headed for the trucks. One young Japanese-American teen stood for a moment, with tears at the corners of his eyes. "Tough luck, Dan," his parents said.

"Sorry," Dan replied as he walked dejectedly away. The old pre-med student had missed his opportunity to join his Hawaiian brothers in the formation of the all-new 442nd Regimental Combat Team.

Service to others was nothing new to young Dan. On December 7, 1941, during the first wave of the enemy attack on Pearl Harbor, the 17 year-old had pedaled his bicycle to the first aid station where he had worked all night and into the next day. In the days that followed he had alternated between studies at school and working a twelve-hour graveyard shift at an aid station. After graduation in the spring, he had enrolled for his first year of college at the University of Hawaii. When the call for volunteers for the new 442nd came out, he signed up the first day.

In the days that followed the announcement of the young men accepted for service, Dan pestered the draft board to learn the reason for his rejection. Finally he was told that because of his continuing work at the aid station, and because he was enrolled in premed studies, he was needed at home. "Give me about an hour," he told the draft board. "Then call the aid station and the university. They'll tell you that I've just given my notice to quit by the end of the week." Two days later Daniel Inouye said goodbye to his family to embark on a wartime military experiment, the outcome of which no one could have predicted.

Though the initial call had been for 1,500 volunteers from Hawaii, in all more than 2,600 young men, most of them Nisei were accepted for service in the 442nd. Back on the mainland, where 110,000 American citizens were being warehoused in concentration camps referred to as "relocation centers," 1,256 volunteered and almost 800 were accepted.

On March 28, 1943 the Honolulu Chamber of Commerce hosted a special farewell for its 2,686 young men leaving for training at Camp Shelby, Mississippi. The Honolulu Star-Bulletin reported:

> "No scene in Honolulu during World War II has been more strik-
> ing, more significant, than that at the territorial capitol grounds
> on Sunday. It was not alone the size of the crowd, somewhere
> between 15,000 and 17,000, and said by old-timers to be the larg-
> est that ever massed within the gateways to old Iolani Palace...
> It was, most significantly, the evident pride of the families and
> friends of these young Americans—their pride that the youths are
> entrusted with the patriotic mission of fighting for their country
> and the Allied Nations."

The recruits of the 442nd arrived at Camp Shelby in May 1943, and began training on the 10th. The unit had been organized into three battalions with supporting Field Artillery, Combat Engineers, Headquarters and Medical detachments. Training began almost immediately upon arrival. The 100th Infantry Battalion had finished most of its advanced training and been sent to Camp Clairborne, Louisiana for the

The Masaoka brothers, Ben, Mike, Tad and Ike

field exercises that would complete its final phase before combat.

By the time the 442nd had completed its first month of basic military training, the 100th concluded their combat readiness training and, after two weeks of rest, returned to Camp Shelby. For many of the young men from Hawaii, it was the opportunity to be reunited with family and friends who had left home to serve their nation a year earlier.

There was no such special reunion for the recruits from the mainland, who had already had more than their share of rivalry with the recruits from Hawaii. Recruits from Hawaii became *buddhaheads*, a slang word deriving its meaning from "pumpkin," much like Americans would use the term to mean a hick from the country. The Hawaiians responded by calling the mainlanders *kotonks*, a term meaning "stone head" based upon a Japanese word used to signify the sound of an empty coconut hitting the ground.

Such rivalries were not unexpected, and as the trainees continued through long hours of combat preparation, they began to come together as a unit. The men of the 442nd would eventually become very much a family, in fact. In some instances they were indeed family, such as was the case of the four mainland Masaoka brothers (Ben, Mike, Tad, and Ike) who all served with the 442nd. The fifth brother in the Masaoka family also served in uniform... with the 101st Airborne.

The rivalries existed not only between the *buddhaheads* and the *kotonks*, however. The new recruits of the 442nd looked with envy at their "brothers" of the 100th Infantry Battalion who had finished training and were ready for action. In July the 100th received its colors, the unit's motto "Remember Pearl Harbor" emblazoned on it for all to see. Shortly thereafter the 100th shipped out to North Africa and then on to Italy. During the "Purple Heart Battalion's" first combat campaign, the soldiers of the 442nd lived in the shadow of the glowing reports of valor and victory amassed by the 100th, while enduring the often tedious and certainly less notable training process. All were eager to finish training and move to Europe to prove that their unit was no less fierce or courageous in battle.

The Department of the Army provided the design for the 442nd's patch with the upraised torch of the Statue of Liberty. Like the 100th Battalion before them however, it was the soldiers themselves that chose the unit's motto.

The dice game of Craps was popular in Hawaii. Those who played knew that in every game of dice there came a point when the game ended and it became time to get serious. In that moment the participant would "go for broke"...risk everything he had... on a single roll of the dice. The creation of the 442nd could have been viewed by some as an experiment, initiated only after a year of calls for an all Japanese-American combat unit. The men of the 442nd bore on their shoulders the hopes of tens of thousands of Japanese Americans who knew their sons, husbands, and brothers were every bit as loyal, tough, and brave as any other young American. The respect rightly due America's Japanese citizens hung in the balance, and the recruits of the 442nd *held the dice*. What they determined to do with those dice became their motto. This was no game; it was serious business that would affect each one of them for the remainder of their lives.

Monte Cassino – War In The Mountains

"We are Iowa boys of the 34th Division, and have fought side by side with the boys of Japanese descent… We know plenty of folks that call themselves Americans that have done much less to prove they give a hang about their country. There have been times when these Japanese, as you call them, have saved many lives, only because they have proven themselves better Americans than some that were not of Japanese descent."

(From a letter to the Des Moines Register written by seven white soldiers of the 34th Division, after they read previous "Letters to the Editor" critical of the Japanese Americans back in their home state of Iowa.")

WHILE THE 442ND was finishing its training at Fort Shelby, the 100th Battalion was fighting for survival in the high Apennine mountains of Italy. The men spent their second Christmas away from home, bundled against the cold blizzards of winter. Slowly some replacements were arriving, often-young Nisei of the 442nd who had completed their training, but the infusion of fresh soldiers could not keep up with the high casualty rate the Purple Heart Battalion was suffering.

It was the aggressive manner in which the Nisei took the war to the enemy, and not a lack of training or leadership that accounted for the high number of men killed or wounded. The Fifth Army had to slug its way to Rome, one heavily defended mountain at a time, and it seemed that the small soldiers of the 100th, dwarfed by backpacks almost as large as they were, were sometimes bent on taking "a mountain a day." On January 11th they took Hill 1109. Two days later they attacked and wrested Hill 1207 from the crack German grenadiers. The next day they moved on to capture Hill 692. The next day they captured the town of San Michele. All this during an intense blizzard that dumped two feet of snow around soldiers with no winter clothing, men who went without sleep for three nights. One of the survivors wrote, "You have to have the will, you have to have the desire, and you have to

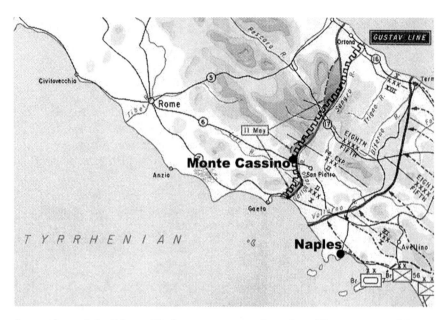

have the spirit. It's a mind over matter situation. You can go without food, you can take extreme cold, you can take extreme heat, you can take anything if you make up your mind you can and you will do it."

In the military history books, one can think of the progress of the 5th Army as being one mountain at a time. To the soldiers who weathered adversity as well as enemy gunfire, rather than being one more mountain gained, it all too often was one more friend lost. One member of the 100th wrote home to say:

> "When you read that a town was taken, or a certain hill was taken, remember that in the process of that accomplishment lives of fine fellows were lost, and also, that during this accomplishment for the participants, life was a horrifying massacre. You lose your buddies—fellows with whom you laughed, ate, slept, sweated. They grow to be more than mere buddies. They become blood relations to you and they die before your eyes—not a pleasant, natural death, but an unimaginable kind of mutilation mixed with groans and prayers ending with a gurgling last breath. Only five minutes ago you might have been laughing with that buddy of yours."

Each mountain the 100th captured also brought them one step closer to Rome, and the goal of liberating the capitol city. One major obstacle loomed in the way of the 5th Army's advance, a high mountaintop crowned with a spectacular monastery. Founded in 529 by St. Benedict of Nursia, it was home to the Benedictine Order. For centuries it had been the preeminent monastery in Western Europe.

Three times it had been destroyed: by the Lombards in 590, the Saracens in 884, and by an earthquake in 1349. Each time it had been rebuilt from the ashes of its ruin. Now the American commanders believed the Germans were using it as a fortress to turn back the 5th Army's advance. Orders came down through the chain of command: Destroy Monte Cassino.

The small town of Cassino sat at the entrance to the Liri valley, blocking the only road north into Rome. German Field Marshal Kesselring had begun to respond to the Allied invasion with a series of tactical retreats further into the mountains. Monte Cassino, the 1703-foot high peak that rose above Cassino, dominated his Gustav Line to check the Allied advance. Into the town, Kesselring poured

Monte Cassino months prior to its destruction in 1944

some of his finest soldiers including the crack 1st German Para-
chute Division. At the top of Monte Cassino stood the ancient and
magnificent monastery. In order to conquer it, The Allies believed
they had no choice but to take it forcefully from the Germans who
controlled it. Reluctant to destroy such a vital part of world history,
British General Bernard Freyberg nevertheless requested permission to bomb the mountain top structure. On February 15th Pope
Pius XII granted permission, and American B17s began dropping
the first of 2,500 tons of bombs to demolish the stone monastery.
They performed their task well, but it was an ill-fated success, for the
rubble of the once elegant monastery provided excellent locations
for the Germans to dig in.

It would take four assaults and cost of over 50,000 casualties to
finish the task the bombers had begun. The blood that stained the
ruins of a once proud icon of world history included the blood of
hundreds of Nisei from the 100th Infantry Battalion.

On the evening of January 20th the 141st and 143d Regiments of
the 36th Infantry Division (formerly of the Texas National Guard)
began crossing the Rapido River, which ran along the side of the
town of Cassino. The ice-choked river was flooding, up to 200 yards
of ground was awash after the Germans had destroyed the dam
upriver. The crossing was made using twelve-man wooden assault
boats. Before the boats were halfway across, German artillery began
to rain from the heavens. Entire boats disintegrated in a flash of fire,
wounded survivors quickly drowning in the frozen waters. By dawn,
only 1,000 men of the 143d had made it across. In the daylight they
came under intense machine gun fire from the German soldiers in
the high ground above them. The regimental commander ordered
them to withdraw, and the haggard remnants of the proud Texas
unit made their way back across the river.

Engineers hastily constructed portable bridges for a renewed crossing, and as night fell on the 21st the soldiers of the 36th moved across
them and into enemy territory, only to find themselves hopelessly
out-gunned with no hope of retreat. Two days of intense fighting followed, but by noon on January 23rd every American on the German

The ruins of the area surrounding Monte Cassino after the bombing assault.

side of the Rapido River had been killed or captured. Three years later the state of Texas asked for a congressional investigation of General Mark Clark and the Fifth Army for committing "one of the most colossal blunders of the war"... an action that almost annihilated two full regiments of the 36th Infantry.

Despite evidence of the powerful enemy force that had repelled two regiments and nearly wiped them out in the previous two and a half days, orders came down for the 100th to cross the Rapido and attack Cassino. The battalion that had landed with more than 1,300 soldiers, had suffered more than fifty percent casualties, and at long last, finally received some replacements. A report on January 20, 1944 listed their ranks as now having 832 men, including officers, which was still well below fighting strength. But orders for the Purple Heart Battalion were to "take Cassino," and the 100th had gained a reputation for following orders, regardless of how impossible the task appeared.

On the night of January 24th the 100th moved into position to cross the Rapido River. Moving out from San Micheli a few miles from the east bank of the Rapido River, the Nisei moved into the darkness. As they approached the river they found themselves in a morass of knee-deep mud caused by the flooding. Embedded in the mud were thousands of deadly German mines. Slowly they moved through the mud, groping in the darkness to detect the enemy mines, they advanced towards the eight-foot high stone dike that channeled the raging waters of the Rapido. At midnight American artillery commenced with a heavy volume of supportive fire that, rather than covering their advance, simply alerted the enemy to their presence. From the high western bank of the river the Germans began to pour deadly machine gun fire on the approaching Nisei from well-hidden and fortified emplacements. Alpha Company's Captain Richard Mizuta was badly wounded probing in the mud for mines, when one of the explosive devices almost severed his right arm and leg. Despite the mud, mines and enemy fire, companies A and C managed to reach the wall, where the men struggled for survival throughout the day.

As night fell on the 25th, Battalion Commander, Major George Dewey, was wounded, and his executive officer was killed as they attempted a reconnaissance of A and C companies. Reassuming command of the 100th was Major Caspar Clough, who had been relieved of command the previous evening for ignoring orders from the regimental commander to send his soldiers into what Clough considered a "suicide mission." The following morning Bravo Company made a daring daylight advance under cover of a smoke screen in an attempt to reach its sister companies. Suddenly the wind arose, blowing away their cover and revealing their position to the enemy in the bunkers on the far bank of the river. Artillery and machine gun fire rained in torrents as the men of B Company struggled through the exploding mines and muddy shore to reach Alpha and Charlie Company at the dike. Of the 187 brave soldiers who began the assault, only 14 reached the wall. They survived only because they had fallen into the mud, lying there as though dead, until darkness fell. As the few survivors of the three Nisei companies hugged the wall in the darkness, regimental headquarters ordered their withdrawal.

The Purple Heart Battalion withdrew to San Micheli to bury their dead, treat their wounded, resupply the survivors, and welcome the few, but not nearly enough replacements. Major Clough had been wounded and the battalion's new commander was Major Jim Lovell who had just returned from a hospital in North Africa where he recuperated from wounds received in a previous action. On February 8th Major Lovell led his men back into action.

Castle Hill (Hill 165) sat over the only paved road leading to the monastery at the top of Monte Cassino. The Purple Heart Battalion took control of the hill against only light resistance, but resistance was strong enough to send Major Lovell home with a war-ending wound to his leg. The recovering Major Clough again took command as the 100th. With virtually no support on its flanks, they managed to cling tenuously to their position. For four days the enemy poured heavy fire on the Nisei. Major Clough was wounded again and two more soldiers were killed in action. Finally, unable to send the beleaguered soldiers support, the regimental commander ordered the 100th to fall back into the hills near Cassino to join the regimental reserves. On February 15th the bombing that destroyed the abbey at Monte Casino began.

After three days of some of the most intense bombing of the war, the second assault on Monte Cassino commenced. It was the last assault on the mountain fortress by the 34th Division, as well as its 100th Infantry Battalion. Already badly decimated by three weeks of fierce fighting, the Division didn't have the manpower to get the job done. One platoon of the Purple Heart Battalion attacked the mountain with 40 soldiers... only to return with five. In four days of intense fighting the 100th managed to fight almost halfway to the top of Monte Cassino, but again there was no manpower left in the Division to render them support. When finally ordered to withdraw the 100th Infantry Battalion was down to 512 men. Monte Cassino remained in German hands, a sad defeat not only for the brave Nisei but also for all the men of the 34th Infantry. Their advance had been strong, aggressive, and nearly successful. Had they not run out of men and material, they just may have succeeded.

It would take five divisions until the 17th of May to finally bring Monte Cassino to its knees. There was no shame in the defeat at Monte Cassino; these brave soldiers had *almost* done it by themselves.

Anzio: All Roads Lead To Rome

"From a cautious experiment the Army has received an unexpect-edly rich reward. A group of sinewy oriental soldiers only one generation removed from a nation that was fighting fanatically against the U.S., was fighting just as fanatically for it."

(From an article in *Time Magazine* in July, 1944)

THE GOAL OF the entire push northward across the Apennine Mountains was the liberation of Rome. Field Marshall Kesselring was determined to prevent the fall of the Italian capitol, and committed his finest troops to battle the Allies. Monte Cassino was the dominant point in his Gustav line, and it had held.

On January 22, 1944, two days before the 100th made its first assault on Monte Cassino, the U.S. 5th Army landed at Anzio, a beachhead south of Rome. The goal was to relieve the pressure at Monte Cassino by placing 50,000 Allied soldiers north of the Gustav line. After the 100th Infantry Battalion's last assault on Monte Cassino, the unit was pulled back into the mountains to recuperate. A month later on March 15th a second wave of bombers, greater than the first, rained tons of bombs on the mountain. The Germans held stubbornly through attacks by five Allied Divisions. Not until mid-May did Monte Cassino fall. Meanwhile, the 100th Infantry found itself stalemated with the other Allied soldiers near the beaches of Anzio.

After their last attack on the monastery on February 18th, the 512 men of the Purple Heart Battalion had pulled back to "heal." Some 200 replacements were brought in, bringing the battalion to almost-half-strength. On March 26th the 100th, moving out of Naples, made an amphibious landing to join the forces of the 6th Army at Anzio.

The Anzio landing, dubbed "Operation Shingle" because it would peel away enemy resistance like shingles off a roof, didn't relieve the pressure at Monte Cassino. Instead, Kesselring sent eight German

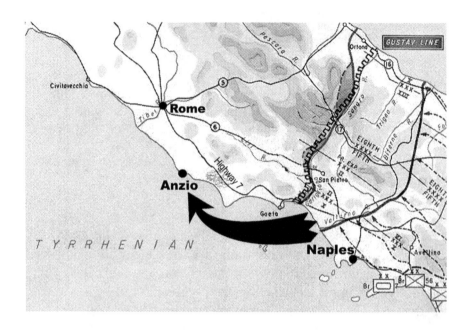

divisions south from Rome to contain the new invasion.

"Containment" is probably as apt a description of those first four months at Anzio as one could find. Winston Churchill referred to the operation as "a stranded whale." After the initial landing in January against light resistance, the battleground became oddly reminiscent of the battlefields of World War One. The Allies had secured a 15-mile beachhead that bulged inward only a few miles. Between the Americans and the German forces was a flat, open "no-man's-land" across which the opposing forces could watch each other through binoculars during daylight hours. Skirmishes were fought under cover of darkness as each side probed the other. When the sun came up the two sides would pull back to their secure areas.

Though both sides launched devastating artillery barrages during the day, there was almost a "gentleman's agreement" between the two sides that no infantry war would be conducted while the sun shined. The men would fight at night, and then relax to eat, sleep and sunbathe during the day. When the men of the 100th recall the two month period after their March 26th landing at Anzio, they often refer to it as their "Dracula Days"... sleeping during the day... drawing blood at night.

This is not to infer that there were no battles, no deaths, and that all was peaceful on the Italian coast. The artillery barrages were devastating, and the efforts to break out seesawed back and forth. The town of Carrocetto changed hands no less than eight times during the four months, as the Allies fought to break out and the Germans fought to contain them.

The fall of Monte Cassino on May 17th was a crushing blow to Kesselring's Gustav line. The Allies now controlled the high ground and the entrance to the Liri valley. It was time to end the stalemate, mount a powerful offensive, and push the last 20 miles to reach and liberate Rome. Once again, it was time for all out war.

Fifth Army military planners selected May 23rd, six days after the fall of Monte Cassino, as "break out" day. The only concern was the lack of intelligence information on the strength and positions of the German units. There was rumor that the enemy ahead was supported by a German Tank Division, carefully camouflaged beyond the no-man's-land. Patrols had been sent out at night to scout the area including one reconnaissance mission by a company-strength probe supported by American tanks.

Not a single enemy soldier had been captured to allow the interrogators opportunity to learn what kind of resistance the May 23rd breakout would face. It seemed to be a problem without a solution, one that could mean disaster to the impending offensive. Once again, the answer came from the 100th Infantry Battalion. This time, it would only take two soldiers to do the impossible. One of them was an officer... the unstoppable Lieutenant Kim who looked the 100th's battalion commander in the eye and said, "Send me out and I'll bring back a prisoner." Lieutenant Colonel Gordon Singles replied "that's crazy."

A blanket covered the window in the second story of the old farmhouse. "Crazy," Lieutenant Colonel Singles thought to himself again, as he moved the blanket slowly aside to peer through his binoculars across the wheat field and barbed wire that marked the no-man's land between Bravo Company and the Germans. The men of Bravo Company usually slept during the daytime, but not on this day... May 17, 1944. In the distance, Lieutenant Young Oak Kim and PFC Irving Akahoshi were slowly crawling towards the enemy. Two men—alone—in broad daylight.

Sometimes it was the crazy ideas that were most successful. So Lieutenant Kim had argued in his bid to get permission to nab a German prisoner. The Korean-born officer of the Purple Heart Battalion explained his plan. The reason, he had told headquarters, that previous patrols had been unsuccessful in snatching a POW were three-fold: First, previous patrols had gone out only at night, when the enemy was most alert. He had watched them through the same second story farmhouse window for days, noted that they came in from night patrols to eat breakfast, and then slept to prepare for the next night's patrols. Secondly, previous patrols had been too large, one even company size. A large a patrol was easy to spot and avoid. Lastly, most patrols did what the enemy expected; taking the routes that afforded the most cover under the blanket of darkness. The enemy would never expect a patrol of two men to crawl through an open wheat field under the bright sunshine, and that was what he and Akahoshi would do.

The previous evening several of Bravo Company's best automatic riflemen had left the safety of the rear staging area at 2200 hours to crawl through the wheat field to the mid-point of no-man's land. Kim had positioned them carefully in foxholes about 0200, then cut a hole in the barbed wire so that he and Akahoshi could slip through into enemy territory. Carrying only a submachine gun, a pistol and a few grenades, the two soon slipped upon an enemy patrol returning to their own staging area. Slowly and quietly the two Americans had crawled more than a quarter of a mile as they followed the enemy. Dawn had broken to reveal the Germans preparing for breakfast. Kim and Akahoshi crawled to a ditch Kim had seen earlier in aerial photographs of the area, and the two men pressed their bodies to the ground and prayed for luck. By 0900 they heard the sounds of snoring as the enemy soldiers bedded down.

Though the soldiers slept during the day, the observers in the nearby enemy outposts would be awake and alert. Kim knew they had to move, skirt the patrol until they could find the right place and moment. Back in the American camp the soldiers anxiously watched the progress. Kim pressed on, praying that he was correct in believing the German observers wouldn't bother to watch their own area. They'd be busy training their field glasses on the Americans on the other side of the barbed wire.

After a nervous two hour crawl around the enemy, Kim and Akahoshi found their prey... two Germans soundly sleeping in a dugout. When the enemy awoke it was to the taste of gun metal. Kim and Akahoshi had carefully placed their submachine guns in the sleeping soldiers' mouths; then awakened them. Removing all weapons, they quietly forced the two to crawl back to the ditch where the Americans had hidden earlier. As dusk began to fall, the four crawled the rest of the way to the barbed wire where the B.A.R. men of Bravo Company waited. Then, with the full darkness of night, the entire patrol returned to the company area.

The two prisoners turned out to be an enemy Sergeant and PFC from a German division's headquarters. The information obtained provided the strategy for the 100th's break out from Anzio a week later. A month later a special ceremony was held to honor Lieutenant Kim and other heroes of the Purple Heart Battalion. On that day General Mark Clark personally pinned the Distinguished Service Cross on Kim's uniform shirt. Then the general stepped back and looked at the Lieutenant again, recognition dawning. Just a few months earlier Clark had presented this same brave lieutenant with a Silver Star. The 5th Army commander called one of his aides, a captain, to his side. He removed one of the aide's parallel silver bars, and pinned them on Kim. Most people, including General Clark, always thought of Kim as being Japanese because of his role with the 100th Infantry Battalion. Captain Kim was the *only* Korean-American to receive the Distinguished Service Cross in World War II.

The break out from Anzio began as scheduled on May 23rd. Thanks to intelligence reports generated by the interrogation of the prisoners captured six days earlier by Kim and Akahoshi, the Fifth

Army chose to make the main thrust through the same area the two soldiers had crawled in their daring feat. Knowing where the enemy was, what his strength was and how best to deploy the Allied troops didn't negate the danger, however, or the fact that every mile to Rome would be a battleground. Once the Fifth Army broke out of the beachhead and crossed no-man's land, they would be faced with forcing a well entrenched German force out of the rugged mountains and valleys.

On May 28th the 7th Infantry was slugging its way through the enemy strongholds near Artena. When a rifle company became bogged down, Staff Sergeant Rudolph Davila, a mainland soldier of Filipino-Spanish descent from Vista, California came to the rescue. moved his machine gunners along an exposed hillside when the enemy opened fire. Davila urged his gunners forward, but they were reluctant in the face of the fierce enemy fire. Sergeant Davila crawled 50 yards to the nearest machine gun, set it up alone, and began returning the enemy's fire. Kneeling in an exposed position in order to maintain accuracy, the brave sergeant stayed in an exposed position firing his gun while enemy bullets bounced off the metal tripod of his gun. Ordering one of his men to replace him at the trigger, Davila crawled forward to direct the fire of his team until both of the threatening enemy positions were destroyed. He brought his three remaining guns forward and commanded and directed their fire until the enemy pulled back.

On the move again, a bullet slammed into Davila's leg. Enemy fire peppered the hillside as the wounded sergeant ignored his pain to run to burning tank. Bullets ricocheted off the hot metal of the destroyed tank as Davila pulled himself to the turret to turn its big gun on the enemy. That done, his attention was drawn to a house 150 yards away from which enemy fire poured down on his men. He forced himself to run to within 20 yards, crawled the rest of the way, and charged into

Rudolph Davila

the building hurtling grenades and firing at the enemy. When the five enemy who had held the house were dead, Sergeant Davila climbed to the attic. The walls were falling apart as fire raked the building. Davila found a large shell hole in the attic and again rained death on the enemy, destroying two more enemy guns and forcing the enemy to abandon their positions. Sergeant Davila was awarded the Distinguished Service Cross for his heroism that day.

Fifty-six years later when President Clinton presented Medals of Honor to 22 Asian-American heroes of World War II, Rudolph Davila was present. One of the 22 awards went to a Chinese-American for heroism in the Pacific. The other 21 awards went to heroic warriors for their heroism in the European theater. Of the many Asian Americans who fought in Italy and France in units other than the 100th/442nd, Davila was the only one to receive the Medal of Honor.

On June 2nd the 442nd Regimental Combat Team landed at Naples to move north and link up with its Nisei brothers. Relief for the 1300-man Purple Heart Battalion that had suffered more than 900 casualties during nine months of combat, was on the way. Before the reunion however, there would be more casualties.

Even as the 442nd was landing at Naples, the 100th was going into battle again. Joined by two artillery battalions, two antitank companies and a chemical mortar company, the 100th was part of "Task Force Singles" led by their battalion commander Colonel Gordon Singles. Their job was to spearhead the drive through Lanuvio and La Torreto, taking the cities and opening Highway seven all the way into Rome. If they were successful the Fifth Army could move swiftly, liberating the city and entering It ahead of the British.

Even as Yeiki Kobashigawa's Nisei brothers of the 442nd were arriving on Italian soil, the 26-year old from Wailua, Hawaii was in the fight of his life. Yeiki was an original member of the 100th. Drafted to

Yeiki Kobashigawa

military service a month before Pearl Harbor, he had been assigned to the 298th Regiment of Hawaii's National Guard. After the immediate hysteria and summary discharge of Japanese-American soldiers that followed the attack, when the 100th Infantry Battalion was organized, Yeiki Kobashigawa had been there. From the battalion's first landing nearly a year before, he had fought his way through the rugged Apennines. Now, as Bravo Company moved against the Germans near Lanuvio, a series of heavily fortified machine gun nests raked the Nisei of his company with devastating fire.

The young sergeant finally spotted one of the enemy positions 50 yards away. With one of his men he crawled forward. With split-second timing he threw a grenade at the enemy position while the other soldier opened fire. Amid the hail of both friendly and enemy fire he charged forward through the smoke and debris of the grenade to kill one enemy and capture two more. When a second enemy position opened up on him, Sergeant Kobashigawa moved forward again, throwing grenades and giving cover fire to the soldier with him who rushed forward to capture the four-man enemy gun crew. Continuing to lead and direct his men, Sergeant Kobashigawa managed to destroy two more enemy gun emplacements.

Fifty-six years after he earned the Distinguished Service Cross, the award was upgraded, and President Clinton hung the blue ribbon of the Medal of Honor around the neck of the 82-year-old war hero.

A short distance away at La Torreto, Private Shinyei Nakamine crawled 175 yards towards an enemy machine gun nest that had caught his platoon in a crossfire. Suddenly he charged, hurtling grenades and firing his submachine gun. Three enemy soldiers fell dead and two others surrendered. The young Army private's first charge of the day had been a success.

A second enemy position fell to the intrepid private later in the day. As other soldiers from his squad provided covering fire, he again rushed forward with grenades to wound one enemy, capture four more, and destroy his second enemy position. A third position would not fall so easily. This time as the brave warrior from Hawaii rushed forward, the men of his squad watched in horror as a hail of enemy bullets abruptly halted his valiant charge. When his DSC was upgraded 56 years later to a Medal of Honor, he was again recognized for destroying an enemy positions that threatened his fellow soldiers.

Shinyei Nakamine

The battle for Highway 7 lasted two days. In the end, Lanuvio and La Torreto fell. From there Task Force Singles moved swiftly through Arricia, Albano, and Fattochie. Fifteen brave soldiers of the Purple Heart Battalion gave their lives in the march to Rome, and 63 were wounded. By the afternoon of June 5th the Task Force had moved within seven miles of the Italian Capitol and the long awaited triumphant entry was in sight. Excitement spread among the men, exuberance at victory, and the thrill of being first to enter and liberate the first European capitol from the Axis.

Then the march was halted, not by the Germans, but by General Harmon of the American First Armored Division. The men of the Purple Heart Battalion were ordered to halt their advance. They sat along the road watching other units march triumphantly down the Highway and into the heroes welcome lavished upon them by the liberated citizens of Rome. It was one of the saddest indignities the men who had fought so hard and given so much could have suffered. Finally, as night fell, a convoy of trucks arrived to transport the weary soldiers of the 100th Infantry Battalion to the outskirts of the city. Years later even the award of the Presidential Unit Citation to the 100th Infantry for its Rome-Arno Campaign (January 22 - September 9, 1945) could not soften the disappointment many of the men felt at the tragedy that befell them on the road to Rome, not by the enemy, but by their fellow Americans.

Reunion – The Rome-Arno Campaign

"In ten months of almost continuous fighting... the 100th Infan-
try (has been awarded)... 1,000 Purple Hearts, 44 Silver Stars,
31 Bronze Stars, nine Distinguished Service Crosses and three
Legion of Merit medals. There has never been a case of desertion
or absence without leave in the 100th, although there were two
reported cases of 'reverse AWOL.' Before their battle wounds were
completely healed in a field hospital behind the lines, two soldiers
left the hospital and hitch-hiked back to their companies on the
battlefield."

From an article in *Army-Navy Register*, August 12, 1944

THE FALL OF Rome was a major coup for the Allies, the first European capitol to be pried from Hitler's control. Though the
men of the Purple Heart Battalion were denied the triumphal entry
they deserved, their exploits had not gone unnoticed by the media.
Repeatedly stories of their courage in battle, their fighting spirit,
and their key role in the advance across Italy graced the front pages
of newspapers and major magazines. Back at Camp Shelby, Mississippi other Nisei read these reports as they finished training with
the 442nd Regimental Combat Team, and to a man they anxiously
awaited the day they would join their brothers in Europe and prove
their own mettle.

That opportunity almost never arrived. Despite the high praise
lavished upon the soldiers of the 100th Infantry Battalion for their
effectiveness in Italy, prejudice and fear still prevailed back in the
states. Unknown to the trainees of the 442nd Regimental Combat
Team and their support battalions, they were being prepared for duty
at home rather than in combat. In the end it was not the exploits of
the Purple Heart Battalion that changed this, but the dedication of
the men training with the 442nd. On the training fields they proved
themselves to be among the best of soldiers, and this admirable repu-

tation led to the unit receiving orders for Italy. Already nearly 400 replacements from the 442nd had been sent to Italy to serve with the 100th, now the entire regiment would make the ocean crossing.

The 1st Battalion of the 442nd remained at Camp Shelby to train new replacements, and was redesignated the 171st Infantry Battalion (Separate). The second and third battalions, along with the 522d Field Artillery and the 232d Combat Engineer and other support companies, would bring the Nisei combat force in Italy to Regimental strength. Upon arrival, the 442nd would absorb the 100th Infantry Battalion to replace the 1st Battalion left at Camp Shelby. After nearly a month at sea, the 442nd arrived at Naples Harbor on June 2, 1944. The same day, further north, Yeiki Kobashigawa and Shinyei Nakamine were battling enemy soldiers in action that would net both Distinguished Service Crosses. (Later to be upgraded to Medals of Honor.) Nakamine's action would cost him his life.

The 442nd made a short sea voyage from Naples to Anzio, arriving two days after the fall of Rome. The 100th had moved on through Rome and northwest to the town of Civitavecchia. It was here that the soldiers of the 442nd finally met up with their brothers, many of whom had spent almost a year in continuous combat. On June 15th the 100th Infantry Battalion was placed under the command of the "Go For Broke" Regiment, as its 1st Battalion. In a highly unusual move, the Army allowed the veteran unit to retain its designation as the 100th Infantry Battalion, due to the record that the unit had built for itself.

All was not joyous in the initial reunion, however. Many of the soldiers of the 442d were upset by the fact that the 100th had re- tained its designation, and felt that the move was an overt display of independence from the parent unit. The soldiers of the 100th were generally older than the new arrivals from Camp Shelby. The men of the 442d were volunteers almost "to a man," while many of the veter- ans of the 100th had been draftees before the war who had returned to service following the initial paranoia that swept the nation. Also, a good portion of the Nisei among the new arrivals consisted of *ko- tonks*, mainlanders... many of whom had enlisted from the relocation camps. For two weeks the veterans of the Purple Heart Battalion had an all too brief opportunity to try and "teach their *kid brothers* from the States the ropes," but it was inevitable that a degree of sibling rivalry would arise.

There was still a very strong German presence in Italy, and a lot of war to be fought. Following the fall of Rome, new enemy troops had arrived to build up the Gothic line north of Florence. Throughout the summer, that Axis force would strengthen its hold, in hopes of holding on throughout the impending winter. For the Allies, the battle north from Rome would be a bitter one. In the process, the men of the 100th and the 442nd led the way. In the process they would learn quickly that, despite their differences, survival depended upon learning to work together. It was a lesson that had taken the non-Japanese in the United States years to learn, a lesson many had still not learned. For the Nisei, they learned quickly that focusing on differences could become a matter of life or death, and it took them less than a month to learn that lesson.

PFC Kiyoshi Muranaga was a *kotonk* who had enlisted to serve with the 442d Regimental Combat Team from the relocation camp at Amache, Colorado. Now, a year after the small built youth had started his training, he found himself battling for his very life near Suvereto, Italy.

It was the first taste of battle for the men of the 442d, and it left an even more bitter taste of fear and desperation. This was not a war maneuver, the bullets weren't blank and the grenades weren't dummies. Everything, including the blood that his fellow soldiers were spilling on the Italian hillside was all too real.

The 442d had started early that morning on the short route to relieve elements of the 517th Infantry Regiment and 142d Infantry Regiment, in an area Major General Charles Ryder, commander of the 34th Division, had been assured was occupied by friendly forces.

Kiyoshi Muranaga

Before the General realized how strong the enemy presence was, his jeep, as well as the jeep of a Colonel accompanying him in the area, was captured. The drivers of both vehicles were wounded, but the General escaped capture himself. It was into the cauldron of such a powerful enemy presence that the raw recruits of the 442d tasted first blood… most of it their own.

The men of the 442d had been anxious to establish their own reputation, to prove they were every bit the warriors their veteran brothers of the 100th had proven to be. For this reason the regimental commander, Colonel Charles Pence, had allowed the second and third battalions to move out at daylight on the road to Belvedere. The 100th was held in the rear in reserve.

Sweeping in along either side of Suvereto just south of Belvedere, they advanced directly into the heavy enemy concentration that held the important Italian city of Belvedere. By early morning the Second Battalion was pinned down by fire from inside the city of Belvedere as well as enemy 88mm weapons hidden in the high hills nearby. Companies E and G were unable to move and taking heavy casualties, including the battalion's operations officer Captain Ralph Ensminger, who was killed in action. Private Muranaga's F Company had been lured into a trap, and found itself under heavy direct fire from a self-propelled 88mm enemy gun.

As the heavy shells began falling on the men of Company F, a mortar squad attempted to set up resistance. The harsh terrain made their effort ineffective, and the soldiers were ordered to take cover. Private Muranaga remained at his gun position, and single-handedly began adjusting mortar fire on the enemy gun.

The enemy position was only 400 yards from the exposed Nisei, but he braved the incoming artillery to drop three rounds near the enemy, adjusting fire each time. His third round landed directly in front of the German 88, causing the enemy to withdraw. Before they withdrew however, they dropped yet another round on the Nisei position. As Private Muranaga prepared to fire a fourth mortar, his position took a direct hit. The young soldier from a Colorado relocation camp became one of the first casualties of the "Go For Broke"

Regiment, earning the Distinguished Service Cross on his unit's first day of battle.

The Belvedere-Sassetta action was the first of three to warrant the award of the Presidential Unit Citation to the 100th Infantry Battalion. By the time it ended the Nisei killed 178 enemy, wounded 20 and captured 86, virtually destroying an entire German SS combat team. It cost the Purple Heart Battalion eleven casualties, including four soldiers killed in action. For the Second and Third Battalions of the 442d, it was a bittersweet introduction to warfare, as the newly arrived soldiers wanted to win their first engagement without any help from their veteran brothers of the 100th.

In the end, it was these battle-savy men who had already fought their way half the distance of Italy's western coast that saved the day. Moving swiftly in from their reserve position, the 100th Infantry moved around to the east of Belvedere. From the high ground north of the city they could see the exposed flank of the German motorized battalion that threatened their brothers in the 2d Battalion. Without protective artillery fire, Company B struck swiftly at the exposed enemy flank, catching it completely by surprise. Company A had moved north to cut off the retreat of the enemy, and Company C followed the enemy into a nearby olive grove to destroy them. By afternoon the road west of Belvedere, which had been expected to require several days of fierce fighting to wrest from enemy control, had fallen to the lightening strike of the 100th.

The previously untested soldiers of the 2d and 3d Battalions had performed well in battle, and had given a solid accounting of themselves. The "rescue" at Belvedere proved that the experience of the veteran Purple Heart Battalion was pivotal to the success of the team, but it also marked the real beginning of the teamwork of all three battalions of the 442nd Regimental Combat Team. It would also foreshadow the 2d and 3d battalion's heroic rescue only six months later in the mountains of France.

The 442d held the area for four days, fighting northward to the Cecina River. On July 1, they crossed the Cecina, the 100th Battalion moving north along Highway 1 to Pisa and the 2d and 3d Bat-

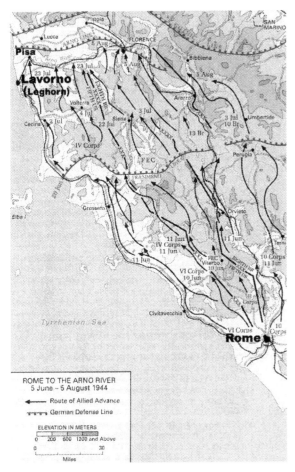

ROME TO THE ARNO RIVER
5 June – 5 August 1944

◄──── Route of Allied Advance
┬┬┬┬┬ German Defense Line

ELEVATION IN METERS

0   200   600 1200 and Above

0   30

Miles

talions fighting their way inland towards Firenze. Both important cities sit on the Arno River and are linked by the east-west Highway 67. The drive to liberate them would remove the Germans from control of the Italian countryside south of the Arno River and bring direct pressure on the Gothic line.

Shortly after crossing the Cecina River, the 2d Battalion began the assault to drive the Germans out of the town of Castellina. Just a week earlier, Company G had been pinned down for most of the day at Belvedere. On the fourth of July they found themselves facing a similar threat. The enemy was dug in on well-fortified hillsides, and suddenly Company G was taking intense fire from several directions. PFC Frank Ono was moving forward with his squad when the torrent began. Quickly he turned his own machine gun on the enemy, knocking out one position with well-placed fire.

Refusing to be pinned down again, PFC Ono began advancing through the merciless hail of lead, killing a sniper and giving his squad leader time to reorganize the squad behind him. The enemy mounted an assault; determine to destroy the lone gunman. PFC Ono felt his machine gun ripped from his grasp by enemy fire. Undaunted he began throwing grenades, defending his position and forcing the enemy back until his platoon moved forward. Then, taking the rifle of a wounded soldier, he renewed his offensive. Suddenly he saw his platoon leader and a rifleman fall nearby. Ignoring the machine gun and mortar fire, PFC Ono ran into the fray to administer first aid. Then, as the platoon was organized to withdraw, the

Frank Ono

young Nisei who had volunteered for military service from Indiana, stayed behind alone to keep the enemy at bay and protect his platoon. Virtually unprotected, exposed to intense fire, and alone, he not only covered the withdrawal of his fellow soldiers, he survived to wear the Distinguished Service Cross awarded for his heroism that day. Mr. Ono never knew his DSC was upgraded to the Medal of Honor. He passed away in 1980 and his award was presented posthumously to members of his family.

Nearby, PFC William "Bill" Nakamura found himself in a similarly perilous position. The twenty-two year old native of Seattle had been attending classes at the University of Washington when Executive Order 9066 ended his academic hopes and placed him at the relocation camp in Hunt, Idaho. There, he had volunteered for service in the U.S. Army, leaving behind the concentration-camp atmosphere for barracks life. Even as Frank Ono fought to save his squad, PFC Nakamura struggled to free his own pinned-down platoon. Alone, he voluntarily crawled toward the enemy gun that kept his fellow soldiers pressed to the ground. Rising within 15 yards of the enemy, he threw four grenades and eliminated the threat. Then

William "Bill" Nakamura

July 1944, (L-R) Edward Nakamura, George Tanna, Suehiko Yoshida,
Mamoru Yonashiro (phone operator) fire a 105 mm Howitzer at enemy positions

he remained behind, again alone, to cover the withdrawal of the platoon. Suddenly he heard the sound of a fierce fire fight. Near the tree line the enemy had opened up on the platoon once again. PFC Nakamura crawled to a vantage point that allowed him to rain effective fire on the enemy, cutting off their assault and allowing the platoon to withdraw into the treeline. As the badly battered platoon from Company G reassembled to regroup and treat the wounded, PFC Nakamura was not among them. His body still lay on the battlefield where he gave his life for his fellow soldiers. He died ironically to preserve the liberties of a nation that only a year earlier had imprisoned him. The date was July 4th, 1944.

The first three Medals of Honor awarded to members of the 442nd Regimental Combat Team all went to *kotonks* in the 2nd Battalion.

Even as the new soldiers were proving themselves to their brothers in the 100th, the mainlanders were showing their comrades from the "Islands" that they had more in common than ancestry. They had a common courage and commitment. More and more the team was coming together. Three days after PFCs Ono and Nakamura wrote new history for the 2nd Battalion, 442nd Regimental Combat Team, Technical Sergeant Ted Tanouye gave the 3rd Battalion its first Medal of Honor hero.

The crest of the hill at Molino A Ventoabbto was vital to control of the vicinity, a strategic position that could control the lower terrain around it. Directed to capture the hilltop, Sergeant Tanouye was moving his platoon forward when he saw five enemy soldiers setting up a machine-gun position from which to attack his own men. Despite the lack of cover on the almost barren hillside, Sergeant Tanouye crept forward alone to destroy the enemy position. As he did, enemy soldiers in a second emplacement located the brave sergeant and began firing at him. Quickly Sergeant Tanouye returned fire, knocking out the second position. Grenades began to rain on the hillside as Sergeant Tanouye moved forward. Heedless of the explosions around him, one of which badly shattered his arm, Sergeant Tanouye moved towards an enemy-held trench, where he again destroyed the German soldiers. He fired until his ammunition was exhausted, then crawled 20 yards to obtain more, and continued his offensive. His leadership and courage inspired his men, and the platoon continued until they had wrested control of the strategic hill from the enemy. Before allowing himself to be sent back for treatment of his wounds, however, Sergeant Tanouye ignored his own pain long enough to organize his men into a defense of the hill they had just taken.

Ted Tanouye

The wounded sergeant would later return to lead his men once more, to fight again for the country he loved, and ultimately to give his life on a foreign battlefield. Tanouye's family

100 Bn. mortar crew fires into hill area where German snipers were last seen.
(left to right) Wallace Higa, James Ishimoto, and Jitsuo Kobayashi

Platoon Leader Lt. Charles Coyne and Sgt. Makoto Taguchi light up while
preparing to leave for reserve after 16 days of hill fighting near Lavorno

later accepted the Medal of Honor on his behalf. At the time of his heroism they prayed nightly for their son, a native of Los Angeles. They remembered him from the spartan accommodations of their temporary new "home" at the Rohwer Relocation Camp.

On that same day, July 7th, the veteran soldiers of the 100th Infantry Battalion that had already endured far too much war, were fighting for survival near Castellina. Each town from the Cecina River was a dangerous battleground, as the rubble of stone houses provided German soldiers with fortified and well-camouflaged positions. Though war continued to be waged on the roads and in the mountains, some of the most dangerous encounters were in the towns. PFC Kaoru Moto was fighting such a battle from house to house when a machine gun opened up on his platoon. He moved to within ten yards of the enemy and destroyed the position. When another enemy opened fire on the Hawaiian soldier, Moto crawled around behind the position to surprise the enemy and capture him. With his prisoner in tow, PFC Moto took a position near a house he believed the enemy would attempt to take and use for an observation post, determined to repulse any attempt by the Germans to enter. While guarding the building, and with a prisoner under his control, he knocked out yet another machine gun position. Wounded by a sniper in another house, PFC Moto dressed his wounds, then made his way back to his platoon. Relieved of his position, Moto was ordered to the rear to have his wounds treated. Even while returning for first aid, the intrepid soldier wouldn't quit. Upon noticing an enemy position near the road, he quickly wounded two, then crawled up to the position and captured these enemies as well.

PFC Moto survived the war to wear his Distinguished Service Cross, but died eight years before his DSC was upgraded to the Medal of Honor.

In the first three weeks of July the 442d Regimental Combat Team was in combat on an almost daily basis, fighting from one town

Kaoru Moto

to the next, pushing the Germans ever closer to the Arno River. The veteran warriors of the 100th Infantry Battalion and their newly arrived brothers of the 442d RCT killed more than 1,100 enemy and captured 331 along the way. It was a 3-week baptism of fire for the green troops from Camp Shelby, but more importantly it was the cornerstone of a developing team that was re-writing military history. They did it through solid tactics, great leadership, personal courage, and an aggressive attitude towards destroying the enemy.

The actions of Company G Staff Sergeant Kazuo Otani on July 15th is perhaps one of the best illustrations of how the soldiers of the Go For Broke battalion welded all these traits together. Sergeant Otani exhibited his great tactical intuition when his platoon was pinned down in a wheat field near Pieve di S. Luce. After killing a sniper, Sergeant Otani ordered his soldiers to crawl to the cover of a nearby cliff, after first making his own desperate dash through a hail of enemy bullets to prove to them that it could be accomplished. While the platoon raced to the cliff for shelter, Otani exposed himself to the enemy, drawing fire away from his men. When part of the platoon reached shelter, Otani organized these men into a defense, and then went back out into the field to encourage the remaining soldiers still stranded to make the dash to a safer area. When one soldier fell wounded, Sergeant Otani crawled forward, completely exposed to enemy fire, to drag the wounded man to shelter. While administering first aid, Sergeant Kazuo was killed by enemy machine-gun fire. Though he would never live to wear his Medal of Honor, his spirit of leadership and concern for his soldiers lived on, as it did among many others like him who fought with the 442d Regimental Combat Team. Though rejected by many of their own nation, these brave warriors worked through their own differences to become not just a team, they grew to became a unique brotherhood.

The three weeks of bitter fighting ended with the liberation of Livorno. This time the Purple Heart Battalion would not be denied the honor due them. The 100th Infantry marched into the town, considered second only to Naples in military importance as a supply base for the Allied Army, preceded only by General Mark Clark in

Troops of the 100th Bn. move through Leghorn (Livorno),
cheered as liberators by local residents

Lt. Gen Mark W. Clark congratulates members of the 442d Regiment after
presenting representatives with a Presidential Unit Citation.

his jeep. General Clark then placed the battalion under direct command of Fifth Army Headquarters, with orders to guard the city and provide order. On July 20th the 2d and 3d Battalions made their own triumphal entry into the historic city of Pisa. On July 25th the 100th/442d RCT was pulled back to Vada on Highway 1 near the Cecina River for rest and recuperation.

While in Vada, General Clark presented the Purple Heart Battalion with the *Presidential Unit Citation* for their outstanding efforts at Belvedere. On July 28th members of the 2d Battalion formed part of the honor guard for His Majesty, King George IV of England. In August Prime Minister Winston Churchill visited the 34th Infantry Division. As he spoke to the soldiers who had fought so hard, for so long, and sacrificed so much... he could not miss those he knew had often led the way... greeting "the Americans of Japanese ancestry and your American officers."

On August 15th, the 2d and 3d battalions' rest came to an end. The soldiers, who had fought so hard to become a team, were separated for a time. The 100th was assigned to the 107th AAA Group, Task Force 45 of IV Corps. The same day the rest ended the 442d's Anti-Tank company was making glider landings on the southern coast of France. The 2d and 3d Battalions of the 442d were relieved from the 45th Infantry and attached to the 88th near Florence. Allied planners claimed the move was an effort to confuse German intelligence.

The reputation of the Nisei had brought them again and again to the attention of the enemy, who tried their best to monitor the movement of one of history's finest fighting forces.

During the last two weeks of August there were more battles like those the Nisei had come to expect, meeting the Germans almost daily in clashes near the Arno River. Even for the 100th near Pisa, the struggle for survival continued. On August 19th an element of Company A, 100th Infantry Battalion was attacked by a large number of German soldiers.

Kazuo Otani

Private Masato Nakae recoiled in horror as a shell fragment destroyed his own machine gun. In the face of an overwhelming force, his weapon useless, he refused to leave his post. Instead he picked up a rifle from a wounded comrade and began firing rifle-grenades at the advancing enemy. As the enemy surged forward determine to take the position by virtue of their superior number, Private Nakae began throwing grenades, ultimately repelling that first assault. A mortar barrage followed,

Masato Nakae

during which Nakae was seriously wounded. Then a second assault was launched. Wounded and suffering intense pain, Masato Nakae refused to leave his position, firing back until the enemy was forced to withdraw. Private Nakae survived the war to return to his native Hawaii, where he died in 1998... two years before he was awarded the Medal of Honor for his heroism that day.

In all, the Rome-Arno campaign cost the 100th/442d RCT nearly 1,300 casualties... one fourth of their total strength. The Nisei buried

The strain of sixteen days of battle is plainly written on the faces of the American troops of Japanese descent, as they leave for regimental reserve.

239 of their brothers, patched the wounds of 972, and remembered in their prayers the 17 men who were missing in action. Their reputation, highly envied, was praised by all. General Ryder himself had watched the Nisei march proudly in a parade during the month of August when Secretary of the Navy James Forrestal visited the Italian front for an inspection. As the men of the 442d marched past, General Ryder turned to the Secretary and said proudly, "My best outfit."

PFC Genkichi Akamine, is a sniper with the 100th Inf. Bn., 34th Division. He has 3 years of service in he U.S. Army, is a native of Hawaii, has fought thru (sic) the entire Italian campaign and just ended sixteen days of hill fighting in the Battle of Leghorn.

The Vosges Mountains: A Different Kind Of War

*"The Nisei bought an awful big hunk of America with their blood.
We cannot let a single injury be done them without defeating the
purposes for which they fought."*

(General Joseph W. Stilwell, speaking against prejudice at home. "Vinegar Joe" was especially enraged by barroom warriors who had never seen combat, but banded together to harass Japanese citizens at home)

O N June 6, 1944, the day after the liberation of Rome, the Allied Forces stunned the Germans when 170,000 soldiers landed at Normandy on the northwest coast of France in *Operation Overlord*. While the 442nd Regimental Combat Team was slugging their way north in Italy from Rome to the Arno River in July and August, Allied forces were pushing eastward in France in the drive to liberate Paris.

The United States Army high command had initially wanted to launch a two-prong assault on France, one from the north (*Operation Overlord*) and one from the south (*Operation Anvil*). Prime Minister Winston Churchill was opposed to the idea, advising vehemently that all available manpower and material be marshaled for the landing at Normandy in the North. In the end, the British prevailed and the June 6th landing took place only at Normandy.

The concept for a landing on the coast of Southern France would not be forgotten. For weeks Allied commanders wrestled with the issue. Proponents wanted a massive invasion from the south that could move up the Rhone Valley via the historic Route Napoleon and become the right flank of the massive Allied movement inland after the breakout from Normandy. On July 15th while Staff Sergeant Otani was in the action that subsequently resulted in his award of the Medal of Honor, the 442d RCT's Anti-Tank Company was pulled back to join the First Airborne Task Force that was training south of Rome

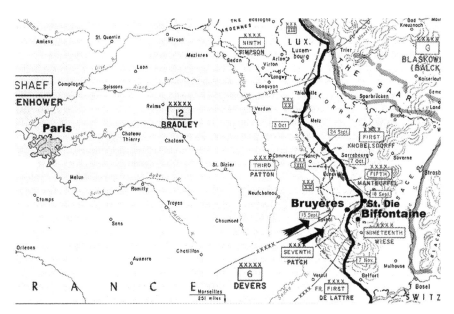

for the invasion of Southern France. On August 15th the Nisei Anti-Tank unit landed with other American forces near Le Muy, France to begin the push eastward to open the Franco-Italian border. Ten days later farther to the north, Paris was liberated.

The Southern France Campaign extended from August 15th to September 14th. During the period the 442d Anti-Tank Company was awarded the Regiment's second *Presidential Unit Citation*. Having made the invasion in gliders and fought with infantrymen of the 6th Army, these soldiers were authorized to wear both the Combat Infantryman's Badge (CIB) and the distinctive Glider Patch on their uniforms.

Operation Anvil was still steeped in controversy and disagreement, so much so that the invasion was re-named Operation Dragoon. General Mark Clark was slated to lead the invasion of South France, but aligned his thinking with that of the British and asked General Eisenhower to allow him to remain with the Fifth Army in Rome. Eisenhower granted the request, but asked the Fifth Army to provide three divisions for the September invasion. Mark Clark quickly provided the necessary forces. He balked only when a second request arrived, asking him to also send the "Japanese-American units".

The campaign in Italy was more bitterly contested than had been anticipated. Military planners had hoped to have almost concluded the effort by the fall of 1944. Instead, the Fifth Army was at a stalemate, facing an immovable enemy force across the Arno line. Such was the situation when the 442nd was relieved near Florence and sent south to Naples to prepare for the invasion of South France. While in Naples the unit received 672 new replacements. The 442d left Naples by transport ship on September 27th, landing near Marseille three days later. From Marseille the 100th and 2nd Battalions moved northward up the Rhone Valley more than 1,000 miles by truck. The 3d Battalion was loaded on a series of old World War I railroad boxcars and sent to join them. Along the way the 442d Anti-Tank Company rejoined the regiment. By October 13th the reunited regiment was only miles from the French-German border, where they were attached to the 36th Infantry, the old Texas National Guard.

The "T-patchers" of the 36th Infantry were a proud lot. They boasted a Texas heritage, though there were certainly many soldiers among them from other states. Private William Crawford of Pueblo, Colorado had been one of the unit's early heroes when he earned the Medal of Honor near Altavilla, Italy. Also earning a Medal of Honor in Italy was a young former gang member from Pittsburgh's north-side tenements named Charles Kelly, forever remembered by his comrades and the media as "Commando Kelly" for his brazen combat heroics.

"T" patch

The "T-patchers" were also no strangers to the Nisei of the 100th Infantry Battalion, next to whom they had fought throughout Italy, most notably in the assault on Monte Cassino. During the disastrous Rapido River crossing, Stephen Gregg had been one of the few members of the nearly devastated 143d Regiment to survive. In that action Gregg had been awarded the Silver Star for heroism. In August the 36th Infantry was reassigned

A team of Japanese-American G.I.'s throwing 105mm shells at Germans in support of an Infantry attack

A column Nisei soldiers file through a wooded area outside Bruyères.

from the Fifth Army to General Alexander Patch's Seventh Army, to make the drive up the Rhone Valley into the Vosges Mountains. The 36th was already battling in France when the 442d left Naples for their Mediterranean crossing. While the Nisei were just one day at sea, Stephen Gregg had added a Medal of Honor to his Silver Star during action near Montelimar France.

Now the Nisei were under the command of the 36th Infantry. Major General John Dahlquist welcomed them happily. He also wasted very little time putting the Regiment to work. On October 15th the 442nd launched their attack on Bruyères. As in Italy, it would be a battle for one hill at a time, moving from position to position. Unlike Italy where the resistance had been fierce, in the Vosges Mountains the fighting would be brutal. They were knocking on the enemy's front door.

On October 15th, the 442d had begun the two-and-a-half mile offensive through the densely wooded Vosges Mountains under orders to liberate Bruyères. With the 3d Battalion in reserve, the 100th began its assault on Hill A, directly west of the town while the 2d Battalion moved in the direction of Hill B to the north. In the first day the Nisei advanced only 500 yards, losing one man killed and 20 wounded. The following morning the two battalions moved into the valley between their respective hills, fighting off a vicious early morning counter-attack by the enemy. On the morning of the October 17th, Companies E and F managed to beat back the Germans before a second counter-attack was launched. Quickly the 100th moved in to shore up the defenses of its comrades in the 2d Battalion. On the morning of the 18th, five artillery battalions laid a 30-minute barrage on the enemy. Four hours of bitter fighting followed, finally allowing the 100th to take control of Hill A. After a similar 7-hour battle, the 2d Battalion took Hill B.

With Hills A and B under American control, the 3d Battalion joined the 36th Infantry's 142d Regiment in the sweep into the city. The battle to take Bruyères had taken three days, and it wasn't over yet. Despite three days of continuous combat, Hills C and D provided the enemy high ground from which to rain artillery down on the city.

(L-R) Abraham Ohama, Kaz Masuda, Zentaro (George) Akiyama

On the 19th the 2d Battalion took Hill C, then moved forward with the 3rd Battalion towards La Broquaine. Soon thereafter, word reached the soldiers that the enemy had counter-attacked, retaking Hill C. Companies F and H were sent back to retake the hill. The fighting was close and heated. Technical Sergeant Abraham Ohama watched as one of his soldiers fell wounded in the open. The sergeant ran forward to render aid, when he too was hit.

During a lull in the firing, the medics moved forward to treat the two wounded. They placed Sergeant Ohama on the stretcher to carry him to safety. As they did, a burst of enemy fire streaked through the mist, shattering the helpless body of the wounded sergeant being carried to safety. As the sergeant died, the full impact of what the other soldiers had just witnessed hit them with a fury. Up to the moments the enemy bullets had struck Sergeant Ohama, the effort to retake Hill D had been a stalemate, a seesaw struggle between the Nisei and the Germans to take and hold each yard. The senseless slaughter of the wounded sergeant sent a ripple of unchecked fury through his men. No order was given for the assault, it was a spontaneous response to what had just happened. To a man the men of Company F rose to their feet with a cry of anger and rushed boldly into the foray, heedless of the danger. The adrenaline charged onslaught quickly turned the stalemate into a rout. Fifty Germans were killed, seven captured, and Hill D once again secured. But for the Nisei it was no longer "Hill D," it became *"Ohama's Hill"*.

Such was the nature of combat in the Vosges Mountains. In Italy it had not been uncommon during a lull in battle for medics from the 442nd to go onto the battlefields under a flag of truce to remove the wounded. The Nisei had extended the same courtesies to the medics of the enemy. But the fighting would be different in France. The Vosges Mountains were the last barrier between the Allies and the Rhine River, the German homeland.

Their backs to the wall, the enemy was under orders to hold the Vosges at all costs. Like a cornered animal, they fought with a ferocity heretofore unseen. There would be no quarter, no mercy.

Added to the desperate resistance of the enemy, the battle in the Vosges would also be fought against the elements. The mountains were covered with thick conifers, heavy undergrowth, and rugged terrain. So thick was the vegetation that the enemy would dig in below ground, watch an American patrol pass within yards of their position, then pop up from hiding to rain death on them from behind. As had been the case in retaking *Ohama's Hill*, the enemy was not always ahead, they were also behind the advance.

With the fall of Hill C to the 100th Battalion the day following the charge at Ohama's Hill, the Americans controlled the high ground around Bruyères. After assaulting and pushing the enemy off the hill under a smoke screen, the 100th was ordered into reserve. They returned reluctantly to Bruyères, knowing there was still a strong enemy presence in the area. The hill they had fought so hard to take fell back into enemy hands when darkness fell after the Purple Heart Battalion's departure on the evening of the 20th. The following morning elements of another American Division approached Hill C, only to find it back under German control. It cost more than 100 casualties to retake the real estate purchased with Nisei blood the day before.

Meanwhile, elements of the 2d and 3d Battalions were stalemated a few miles east at the important rail center of La Broquaine. Because the enemy was behind as well as ahead of the advancing Nisei, evacuation of wounded to the rear and the flow of supplies to soldiers in the forward areas was often difficult and dangerous.

On October 20th one supply train was attempting to shuttle needed

ammunition and supplies forward when it
was ambushed by a strong enemy force. Staff
Sergeant Robert Kuroda was leading his
squad in an effort to destroy the snipers and
machine gun nests in the hills when the supply
train was pinned down by fire from a heavily
wooded slope. Ignoring the deadly fusillade
around him, Sergeant Kuroda advanced to
the crest of the ridge where he located an
enemy emplacement. Within 30 feet of the
enemy he began hurling grenades and firing

Robert Kuroda

clip after clip of ammunition, destroying the position, and killing
at least three enemy soldiers. As his ammunition was exhausted,
he saw an American officer fall to the enemy hail. Sergeant Kuroda
ignored the heavy fire to rush to the aid of the officer. The officer
was dead, killed by fire from an enemy position on an adjacent hill.
Sergeant Kuroda took the fallen officer's Tommy gun and turned
it on the enemy position, advancing until it fell quiet to his fearless
charge and accurate fire. Slowly the Sergeant turned towards the
sound of additional enemy gunfire, seeking to locate the position. As
he prepared to turn his submachine gun on the position, a sniper's
round streaked through the hillside, ending his valiant rescue of the
supply train. For his heroism, H Company's Staff Sergeant Robert
Kuroda was posthumously awarded the Distinguished Service Cross.
Fifty-six years later it was upgraded to a Medal of Honor.

THE SMALL FRENCH villages in the Vosges are only a few miles apart, but
because of the terrain they can appear far removed from each other.
They can almost seem isolated from each other by the thick forest. In
the early winter, the weather causes them to seem even further apart.
It rained on October 15th when the offensive towards Bruyères began,
continued to rain almost constantly for the next ten days as the 442d
battled from one hamlet to the next. In the early morning the moist
ground yielded a dense fog, making travel even more difficult.

The 36th Infantry's 141st and 143d Infantry regiments, as well as the three battalions of the 442nd regiment, were scattered throughout the small region. Because of the terrain, the weather, and the fog, it was often difficult for the units to keep track of who was where. Companies I and K were pursuing the Germans who were withdrawing from Bruyères into the Belmont forest. Though in retreat, the enemy still fought furiously. Among the Nisei killed pursuing the enemy was a young soldier from Los Angeles, Technical Sergeant Ted Tanouye who would never know he had earned the Medal of Honor less than 100 days earlier in Italy.

Meanwhile, Company K had found a complete set of the German defense plans for the region on the body of an enemy officer killed in a skirmish with a German armor column. This led to the formation of Task Force O'Connor, consisting of Companies F and L, and led by 3d Battalion's Executive Officer Major Emmet O'Connor. Task Force O'Connor, bolstered by the new intelligence information, moved out at dawn the following day along the left flank of the 2d and 3d Battalions. After fierce fighting, the task force closed ranks with their comrades in a pincer movement that virtually secured the area from Bruyères to La Broquaine by the evening of October 21. Along the way the task force killed 80 enemy soldiers, captured 54, sent most stragglers deeper into the Belmont Forest, and earned a *Presidential Unit Citation* for the two companies.

After being ordered back to Bruyères from Hill C, the 100th Battalion bedded down in the city. Early in the pre-dawn hours of October 21, as the weary soldiers of the Purple Heart Battalion tried to rest, the unstoppable Captain Kim joined Colonel Singles at Battalion headquarters. The assistant division commander had arrived with new orders: "prepare to move out for Biffontaine."

The small French hamlet in peacetime boasted a population of some 300 people, living in homes nestled among the hills of the Vosges. Now much of it was deserted, save for the Germans who had fortified a position near the village church. Without so much as a full night's sleep, the Nisei of the Purple Heart Battalion were rousted for a quick, forward movement. In the hours before dawn they nearly ran as they forced their way to a ridge overlooking Biffontaine. In the process they passed through the enemy defenses, only to find themselves

Nisei combat team moves through French village

isolated by early morning, cut off from the rest of the 442d.

As night fell on the 21st, the brave but weary warriors were low on ammunition and supplies. For many there had been no food rations in more than 24 hours. The soldiers clasped hands over their empty stomachs, counted their rounds, and dug in for the night.

Early the following morning the 100th began digging the enemy out of the area. The Nisei were taking fire from three sides, and their meager supplies were almost gone. The battalion S-3 sent a report stating: "The 100th will have to be throwing stones if they don't get ammo." One supply train from Company A was ambushed by 50 Germans. Captain Kim and his other officers would have been content to sit on the ridge and hold the line until they could obtain resupply and reinforcements. Any other action may have been foolish, and foolishness indeed prevailed!

"Capture Biffontaine," was the order transmitted from the division to the officers of the 100th.

"This puts us beyond radio range and artillery support, and we are low on ammunition," Captain Kim responded over the radio.

"Promise that you'll put another unit in our position (on the ridge overlooking Biffontaine) if we go down into Biffontaine." The regimental commander promised. And with that, the battered Nisei fighting force began sliding down the steep slopes of the ridge and into the city.

Fortunately, most of the Germans that had been holed up in the city had already escaped the "back way." Only about 50 Germans remained behind, unable to make the withdrawal. Biffontaine fell easily to the *Purple Heart Battalion*. It would not be held so easily. Rather than leaving the town to the Allies, the Germans attacked from four directions, moving in on the Nisei. One emerging German fired several rounds at Captain Bill Pye, Commander of Charlie Company. He missed the CO, the bullets flying under the officer's arm as he pointed to the enemy. Three of the whispering shards of death slammed into Captain Kim's right hand. While the soldiers tried desperately to hold in the face of the German counter attack, help was on the way.

The Felber task force, consisting of an armored group, set out from Belmont to bring fresh water and ammunition to the surrounded Nisei at Biffontaine. From the high ridge that separated the two towns, (the same ridge held by the Nisei at the time they were ordered into the village) German fire halted the supply train. The Second Battalion was pulled from reserve and sent to the rescue. As they struggled towards their surrounded, outnumbered comrades, their flank was hit by a special detachment of German bicycle troops. The advance to Biffontaine slowed, but the infantrymen of the 442d beat back the superior firepower of their highly mobile opponents.

Company K of the Third Battalion moved along the floor of the valleys to dig out the enemy and fight their way into Biffontaine. Troops from Company G of the 2d Battalion were moving on foot under the leadership of the battalion S-4 Captain George Grandstaff, carrying supplies to the beleaguered force at Biffontaine.

The fighting was incessant, one ridge at a time, one more yard gained, yesterday's accomplishments quickly forgotten in the challenges of today's. Three days earlier Private Barney Hajiro of Hawaii had distinguished himself near Bruyères by exposing himself to an enemy gun emplacement to draw their fire away from other troops attacking the position. He had quickly killed two enemy snipers bringing a much-needed relief to the attacking Americans. That was three days before, miles behind his current position where on October 22d he and another soldier concealed themselves to ambush an enemy patrol. Together, the two men killed two, wounded one, and captured the remainder. Today's fierce fighting and Private Hajiro's heroic action would not al-

Barney Hajiro

low himself a moment to relax and ponder his accomplishments as a soldier. The 18-man enemy patrol was only one of hundreds that moved through the forests of the Vosges Mountains.

Late in the day the Germans launched a second counter-attack at Biffontaine, supported by tanks. None of the resupply/reinforcement efforts had yet succeeded. The men of the Purple Heart Battalion would have to hang on by sheer force of their own will. As darkness fell, the enemy had moved infantry and armor into the city, proclaiming, "You are surrounded." The rifle fire and grenades of Nisei who refused to quit met their calls for surrender. As darkness fell on the 22nd, the 100th Infantry Battalion was still surrounded in a city they shared with the enemy. The house-to-house battle ranged into the night.

Before the sun arose on the morning of October 23d, an attempt was made to send out a party of wounded under Lieutenant Jimmie Kanaya. Six guards were assigned to protect the eleven wounded men that included Captain Kim. Morphine had dulled some of the brave Korean's pain, but it had also dulled his senses and created some disorientation. The wounded that could not walk were carried on stretchers by a group of 20 German prisoners of war. As the small contingent moved through the dark forest, they paused momentarily to rest. Suddenly a squad of enemy confronted them. The Nisei called for the enemy squad to surrender. At first it seemed the ruse would work, then the world caved in. Captain Kim and Private Richard Chinen, a medic, managed to make it into the woods in an effort to evade the enemy. The badly wounded Kim and the medic were the only men of the litter detachment to escape capture. Kim would reach safety and have his wounds treated, but his war was over. Also lost to the leadership of the 100th Battalion was the Captured Lieutenant Kanaya and Alpha Company Commander First Lieutenant Sam Sakamoto. The latter had been evacuated on a stretcher after being severely wounded in the back, when the Germans captured him.

With virtually no officers to command them and no resupply in two days, the men of the Purple Heart Battalion struggled to hang on through the morning of the 23d. The Germans launched a third brutal assault on Biffontaine. The Nisei were reduced to fighting back with weapons taken from the dead bodies of their enemies. Miraculously they held, forcing the enemy to withdraw. By afternoon the 3d Battalion took control of the ridge overlooking Biffontaine. Task Force Felber broke through with water and ammunition and, more importantly, reinforcements for the battered city. The Germans had lost Biffontaine, along with 40 men killed or wounded and another 40 captured. It had cost the Purple Heart Battalion 21 soldiers killed, 122 wounded, and 18 captured.

The casualty numbers didn't reflect the loss in leadership for the 100th. In addition to Kim and Lieutenant Sakamoto, Bravo Company's Captain Sakae Takahashi had also been wounded. The entire 442d was pulled back to Belmont to lick its wounds and mourn its dead. As night fell on October 24th, the venerable unit could look back proudly on eight days of continuous combat under the most untenable of conditions. Badly battered, their ranks severely depleted, they had survived the enemy, the elements, and a series of bad decisions by division headquarters. Now, at last, they could rest for a few days, maybe even a week.

Unknown to the Nisei in that moment was the predicament faced by the 3d Battalion, 141st regiment of 36th Infantry more hopelessly surrounded than the Purple Heart Battalion had been at Biffontaine. Nine miles into enemy territory, every effort had been expended to save them... all to no avail. To call the battered 442d back into action so soon would be to sign the death warrant of a legendary battalion. But when all else had failed the stranded T-Patchers were left with only one hope of rescue.

The Lost Battalion – Rescue in the Vosges Mountains

"Greater love hath no man than this, that a man lay down his life for his friends."

The Holy Bible, John 15:13

VETERANS OF THE 442d Regimental Combat Team take great pride in the accomplishments of their unit. Still, many often refer to their role in World War II as being "cannon fodder" for the Germans. Whether this perception is accurate or not, the events in the Vosges from October 15th to the 30th certainly gave the brave soldiers cause to believe it was true.

In Italy the Purple Heart Battalion had become renown for suffering a record casualty rate. In Italy, however, the Nisei had believed there were clear-cut objectives to be purchased with their blood and their sacrifice. At Monte Cassino they had watched non-Japanese units, such as the 36th Infantry's 141st and 143d Regiments nearly decimated right next to them. In France where the rain and fog in the Belmont forest obscured the terrain, in the Vosges Mountains many of the brave Nisei felt their orders and objectives were vaguely defined.

From October 15-24, each Company had been thrown, almost in a scattered "shot-gun" pattern, at numerous hills and positions, with what they often felt was little clear-cut reason. Frequently, as had been the case with Hill D, once they had purchased a position with their blood, they were moved on to the next assault only to watch hard-earned acreage fall back into enemy hands due to poor planning at the division level.

The outspoken Captain Kim had always stood up for the men, never defying orders, but often questioning them or offering more reasonable alternatives. When rousted in the early morning hours of October 21 and ordered to move his weary soldiers into the ridge above Biffontaine, Kim had dutifully followed orders. He didn't understand the reasoning behind them, indeed walked back to his jeep muttering, "This is crazy. This is crazy." But, like all the men of this unit (the only World War II unit to be able to claim zero battlefield desertions during the war), he followed orders. As the weary regiment bedded down at Belmont on October 24 for what they hoped would be at least the two-day rest period they'd been promised, Kim was gone, recovering from his wounds at Biffontaine.

There must come, at some point in time, a limit to the endurance of the human spirit, mind, and body. The Bruyères-Biffontaine campaign had certainly pushed the young Nisei to that point. For days they had tasted fear as they met the enemy, and watched their comrades mutilated beyond recognition by enemy machine gun and artillery fire. Struggling to survive with few supplies and little support, the unwounded soldiers of the 442d bedded down at Belmont also carried scars deep inside their souls. To add to their misery, the rain had been almost constant throughout the previous eight days of combat. Every man was soaked to the skin, the constant moisture turning flesh white and wrinkled. The constant movement through the cold mud of the mountains had kept feet from drying for more than a week. A new threat became as real as the armed enemy... trenchfoot... far worse than athlete's foot for it could not only immobilize a foot soldier, it could cost him his leg.

The campaign had also been costly for the enemy, 645 Germans captured and at least an equal number killed or wounded. It had been a bitter defeat for them, right at their own doorstep. At the American Army's Corps level it was determined that enemy resistance west of the Meurthe River had been effectively crushed. Military planners at headquarters determined that the time was ripe to send the 3d Division, which had been in rest for ten days, in a push to reach the Meurthe River from St. Die. Further south, the 36th Infantry was ordered to move east of Biffontaine to protect the 3d Division's right flank. Even as the 442nd was pulling back to Belmont to heal, a unit consisting of Company A, Company B, and a portion of Company C (as well as one platoon from Company D) of the 1st Battalion, 141st

Regiment of the 36th Infantry Division was moving eastward from Belmont to fulfill this task. Joining the 274 T-Patchers was First Lieutenant Erwin Blonder, an artillery observer.

The 1st Battalion had moved out with dawn on October 24th, moving down a thickly wooded valley between Gerardmer and St. Die to rout the enemy from their hidden positions. By mid-afternoon the soldiers had traveled nearly six miles into enemy territory, flanked by 3d Battalion on a ridge to the north. Rising from the valley, the 1st Battalion attacked the heavily wooded hillsides, beating back the Germans. Suddenly the enemy counter-attacked, splitting the two Battalions and cutting the 1st Battalion off from its flank support.

As night fell, 1st Battalion had taken a position on the barren crest of the densely wooded hilltop. As they prepared for the long night, the battalion's three Lieutenants under Lt. Blonder held a war council. Together with the NCOs, they asked each soldier to empty his pack, counting rations, supplies, and ammunition, and then distributing them equally among the men. So far forward was the unit that transmissions to the rear were scratchy and barely audible on Lieutenant Blonder's radio. The officers could only hope that headquarters understood the coded message sent back that first night: "No rations, no water, no communications with headquarters... four litter cases." As desperate as the situation sounded, the officers of the 1st Battalion did not realize yet just *how* critical their situation was.

First Sergeant Bill Hull sent a 36-man patrol to work their way back to friendly lines and obtain needed supplies for the men on the hilltop. Almost immediately after leaving the perimeter, the patrol ran into the Germans. The first hint of just how badly surrounded the 1st Battalion was, came when only five of the 36 escaped to return to the hilltop. In the darkness of that first night, the soldiers took turns standing guard duty. But no one really slept. They knew the enemy was near, that they were surrounded. They suspected that they were also heavily outnumbered.

They were indeed. Stinging from their defeat in the Belmont forest, the Germans had rushed a massive number of fresh troops into the region. During that first night it was later estimated that some 700 enemy soldiers moved in to surround the 1st Battalion. At 1000 hours the following morning the enemy revealed their presence. Slowly a lone German tank moved through the forest to confront the American soldiers huddled in their small, muddy perimeter. As the enemy began the frontal attack, the T-patchers met it with a hail of machine gun fire. When the initial fusillade died down, the tank withdrew. It had simply been a probe, an effort by the enemy to determine the strength of the surrounded Americans. The charade would continue daily, almost like clockwork... a frontal assault by a lone German tank. Each time the Americans met it with a hail of bullets, all the while knowing their supply of ammunition was depleting with each engagement.

Most felt that the only reason the Germans had not yet attacked in force was because they weren't sure how many Americans were on the hill. Any sign of weakness, any lessening of the full resistance necessary to convince the Germans that they were up against a powerful Allied unit, would result in the battalion's immediate annihilation.

Throughout the day the soldiers continued to reinforce their position, digging foxholes into the ground and using knives to cut down trees for cover. Every effort was made to maintain silence, for the Germans seemed to be everywhere. Some of the soldiers resorted to wrapping blankets around small trees as they cut through the trunks, in order to quiet them as they fell.

Back at headquarters, Major General Dahlquist, Commander of the 36th Infantry Division, was concerned. The situation faced by the 275 men he had sent from Belmont posed potential for a major military disaster. Throughout the previous night, the 3d Battalion of the 141st had tried to fight their way past the forces that had stopped 2nd Battalion from reaching the trapped unit. It was all to no avail. Quickly the Americans were learning how strong the reinforced German defenses had become.

"Hang on, a heavy force is coming to relieve you," headquarters radioed back to Lieutenant Blonder.

With his staff, General Dahlquist had committed all the resources of the 2d and 3d Battalions to the situation. Dahlquist also hoped to determine what kind of manpower would be required to push through to the lonely hill, where the majority of his 1st Battalion was huddled against the powerful German force. On the hillside, the enemy was moving in more tanks, heavy guns, and dropping artillery fire on its cornered prey. In the forests they were blocking the advance of the American relief efforts. The 1st Battalion wasn't really "lost," the Germans knew where they were, and so did General Dahlquist. But

*Major General
John E. Dahlquist*

knowing where the trapped unit was, and affecting their rescue, were completely different issues. Huddled in the mud protecting the radio that provided the Lost Battalions' only link to the rear, Lieutenant Blonder prayed for a miracle.

Back in Belmont, weary Nisei who had already been pushed beyond the limit of human endurance were rising up to do the impossible. Sometimes when you go for broke, you win big. At other times the roll of the dice can be cruel, and rob you of everything. This time the roll of the dice would be insanely cruel, for men who refused to quit, refused to lose!"

COLONEL CHARLES PENCE knew something major was up the minute General Dahlquist walked into the 442d RCT's command post at Belmont. The RCT commander wasn't surprised to see the division commander, visits from the General and his crisp aide Lieutenant Lewis, were common. Today, however, Colonel Pence's attention was quickly drawn to the other officer with General Dahlquist. It was hard to miss the three stars on the uniform of Lieutenant General Alexander Patch, commander of the 7th Army Corps. Yes, something was definitely in the wind.

"I don't really want to send your soldiers to battle again, so soon,"

Infantrymen hike up a muddy French road to their new bivouac area.

General Dahlquist told Colonel Pence, "But I have little choice." With that, he ordered Second Battalion to move out before darkness fell, to assume a defensive position on the flank of the 141st Regiment. From there, the General visited Lieutenant Colonel Singles at the 100th Battalion's command post. He laid out the scenario being played out on the hilltop near La Houssiere, explaining the predicament of the Lost 1st Battalion and informed the Purple Heart Battalion's commander to have his soldiers ready to move out on a moments notice, should it be necessary to commit them to the rescue effort.

The 100th and the 3d Battalions remained for one more day at Belmont as the exhausted men of the 2d Battalion moved out in support of the 141st Regiment. As dawn broke the skies on Thursday, October 26th, the Lost Battalion had survived its second night on the hill. The beleaguered soldiers were under almost constant enemy artillery fire and most had not eaten in 24 hours.

Meanwhile, for two days the enemy had pushed back every effort by the remainder of the 141st Regiment to reach their trapped comrades. East of Belmont, Technical Sergeant Charles Coolidge was covering 3d Battalions right flank. His subsequent Medal of Honor citation explains much of the difficulty the "Texas Division" encountered:

> *Coolidge, leading a section of heavy machine guns supported by one platoon of Company K, took a position near Hill 623, east of Belmont sur Buttant, France, on 24 October 1944. His mission was to cover the right flank of the 3d Battalion to support its action. T/Sgt. Coolidge went forward with a sergeant of Company K to reconnoiter positions for coordinating the fires of the light and heavy machine guns. They ran into an enemy force in the woods estimated to be an infantry company. T/Sgt. Coolidge, attempting to bluff the Germans by a show of assurance and boldness called upon them to surrender, whereupon the enemy opened fire. With his carbine, T/Sgt. Coolidge wounded two of them. There being no officer present with the force, T/Sgt. Coolidge at once assumed command. Many of the men were replacements recently arrived; this was their first experience under fire. T/Sgt. Coolidge, unmindful of the enemy fire delivered at close range, walked along the position, calming and encouraging his men and directing their fire. The attack was thrown back. Through 25 and 26 October the enemy launched repeated attacks against the position of this combat group but each was repulsed due to T/Sgt. Coolidge's able leadership. On 27 October, German infantry, supported by two tanks, made a determined attack on the position. The area was swept by enemy small arms, machine gun, and tank fire. T/Sgt. Coolidge armed himself with a bazooka and advanced to within 25 yards of the tanks. His bazooka failed to function and he threw it aside. Securing all the hand grenades he could carry, he crawled forward and inflicted heavy casualties on the*

advancing enemy. Finally it became apparent that the enemy, in greatly superior force, supported by tanks, would overrun the position. T/Sgt. Coolidge, displaying great coolness and courage, directed and conducted an orderly withdrawal, being himself the last to leave the position. As a result of T/Sgt. Coolidge's heroic and superior leadership, the mission of this combat group was accomplished throughout four days of continuous fighting against numerically superior enemy troops in rain and cold and amid dense woods.

The men of the 442d's Second Battalion were ordered to move out in front of the 141st's Third Battalion. Though the Nisei themselves were not yet aware of the plight of the Lost Battalion or the reason for the move, it was the first step in a series of actions that would place the fate of Lieutenant Blonder in the hands of the Go For Broke regiment.

Lieutenant Blonder knew the men were getting desperate. It was possible to survive for a period without food, but the men needed water. When possible, rainwater was collected from shell holes on the hilltop. Further down the hill was a larger pond that had accumulated considerable water from the incessant precipitation. The water was green and foul tasting, but it was water. At night the Americans would try to slip through the forest to haul back the much-needed water. They did so with their weapons gripped tightly, their senses alert. The Germans controlled the forested sides of the hill, and drew water from the same hole.

Back at Belmont, at 2:00 a.m. on October 27, the two remaining battalions of the 442d Regimental Combat Team were alerted. Two hours later the 3d Battalion moved out and into the darkness of the forest. An hour later the 100th Battalion followed. Every other effort to relieve the Lost Battalion had failed. Now it would be up to a group of soldiers who only two days rest after more than a week of unrelenting combat, to accomplish what no one else seemed able to do. Still the Nisei were not aware of the nature of their mission, the lives that depended upon their success. But as they moved out of Belmont it was hard to miss the line of ambulances and built up aid stations that

*Japanese-American's medics take a break near an
advance aid station near Belmont*

had been assembled for the eventual rescue. It was an eerie symbol of what lay ahead.

Moving into the forest, it was almost impossible to see. The soldiers created a human chain, each man holding the straps of the pack ahead of him. Sliding down muddy trails, forcing their way through dense brush, and stumbling over sharp rocks, the Nisei walked obediently into the jaws of certain death.

All three battalions moved slowly northward in the direction of St. Die, to approach the La Houssier position from the northwest. Third Battalion, already far forward, would make the drive down the middle with the 100th and 2d Battalions guarding the flanks. On that first day, a heavy concentration of German 88mm fire tore into the men of the 3d Battalion, causing numerous casualties. Still, the brave men fought on. In the forests, the Germans seemed to be fighting with increased intensity. The German high command had become aware that their soldiers in the Vosges had trapped nearly an entire American battalion and Hitler had personally issued orders to stop any rescue effort.

The three battalions of the 442d spent their first full night back in the forest trying to hold their positions and stay alive. Their orders were to attack at daylight, in what General Dahlquist expected to be an aggressive and swift push to snatch the Lost Battalion out of harms way.

During the night the enemy moved reinforcements, including heavy armor into the valley to turn back the Americans. When the attack commenced at 0630, it was still dark in the forest. Suddenly the darkness came alive with the brilliant flashes of enemy artillery. Company K took two hours to push forward some 350 yards when an enemy mortar left several brave soldiers lying in the mud, dead and dying. By mid-morning platoon sergeant George Nishi was the only NCO left in the unit. As he attempted to pull his men back, a grenade landed in his foxhole. Quickly he tossed it back at the enemy. A second grenade came in his direction, killing the young soldier behind him. Nishi was wounded in the back.

Shortly before noon, after receiving orders from General Dahlquist, Colonel Pence ordered Company L out of reserve. The division commander was desperate; the loss of the Lieutenant Blonder and his "Lost Battalion" would be a major catastrophe. Not only did the General order an unrelenting frontal assault by the 442d regardless of cost, he went to the front himself, issuing orders and pushing men forward. To many of the Nisei, none of whom still were aware that their mission was one to rescue a lost battalion of friendlies, it was senseless. It was difficult to see themselves as anything other than cannon fodder, expendable in the push through the Vosges.

The battle raged through the morning. Artillery support was requested. On the right flank the 100th battled through the forest. First Lieutenant James Boodry, the battalion S-3, was killed by an airburst as he huddled next to Charlie Company Commander Bill Pye mapping out the forward strategy of the battalion. Boodry had replaced Kim when the latter was wounded at Biffontaine by bullets meant for Pye. The same shrapnel that split open the head of Lieutenant Boodry also wounded the Charlie Company commander. Reeling in horror, blood streaming from his wounds, Pye moved forward. Minutes later the fierce enemy fire reached out to him again. He would go no further into the Vosges, one leg shattered by an enemy shell.

Everywhere, casualties were falling... to enemy fire... to artillery fire... to mines and booby traps. Technician Fifth Grade James Okubo was a medic. All the medics of the 442d had gained the respect of the soldiers time and again, going into the open to recover wounded, hoping that the enemy would respect their non-combatant status. Sometimes it worked... sometimes it didn't. As the Nisei advanced on the enemy, they were faced with minefields and roadblocks, behind which the enemy could hide and rain artillery on the advancing Americans. One hundred fifty yards ahead of Okubo lay wounded soldiers, within 40 yards of the enemy lines. Despite the heavy fire he crawled forward time and again. Two grenades landed near him but he ignored the danger they represented. In all he rescued and treated seventeen men.

As darkness fell again over the forest, even Lieutenant Colonel Singles was wounded. The same shell that peppered his body with hot metal as it struck his jeep had killed the passenger next to him and wounded another. After two days of horrible fighting, two lieutenants were all that remained to command the entire battalion. During the night a patrol of twelve men was sent through the darkness to the rear to obtain badly needed ammunition and supplies. The patrol was unable to finish their important task. Two were killed and the remaining ten were wounded.

Lieutenant Blonder huddled next to the radio as dusk fell on the battalion's fifth night alone on the barren hilltop. Freshly

James Okubo

turned dirt revealed the place where earlier in the day, his men had buried three more of their own. He had made it a practice to send out only two radio messages each day in an effort to spare the battery of the one precious link the men had with the rear. His messages were always a variation of the same message:

> *"Send us medical supplies...We need rations... Please, we need fresh water... I need radio batteries... My wounded need plasma."*

Every morning the enemy tank had appeared. Throughout the day and night, enemy artillery fell on their small 350-yard defensive position.

During the day a flight of P47 fighter-bombers of the XII Tactical Air Combat Wing flew over to drop supplies. The stranded soldiers on the ground waved white underwear and popped smoke grenades to guide them in. None-the-less, few of the supplies landed in the small perimeter, and much of the supplies that were on target quickly rolled down the hillside and into the hands of the enemy.

That evening an American 105 mm artillery round whistled through the air, homing in on top of the men of the Lost Battalion. Buried in the nose of the warhead in place of explosives, was chocolate. It was a bizarre, desperate effort to get some nourishment to embattled soldiers who had not eaten in a week. The velocity of the shell caused the chocolate to burrow deep into the mud upon impact. It was a novel idea, a good effort, but like all other efforts to provide relief to the Lost Battalion, it had failed.

The survivors on the hillside had no way of knowing that the men of the Go For Broke regiment were slugging their way to reach them. They could only hope and pray that the next day would bring familiar faces breaking through the forest below them. With dawn they would face their sixth day alone in enemy territory. Though they prayed that day six would bring rescue, instead it would only bring the worst yet... both for the men on the hill and the brave Nisei coming to their rescue

It wasn't until October 29, almost a week into the rescue mission, that the men of the 442d Regimental Combat Team were made aware of the fate of the Lost Battalion and of the purpose of their mission. With that knowledge came some understanding of the events of the previous days. For the men of the 100th who had been cut off and surrounded at Biffontaine, there was a special sense of identity with Lieutenant Blonder and his men. It steeled the resolve of the surviving Nisei to push forward. It also helped to explain the division commander's frustration and drive in the field.

The men of the 442nd knew that General Dahlquist, despite all his perceived shortcomings in the way he used the Nisei unit, did not lack in courage. Field commanders had become accustomed to seeing top brass in the field on occasion. They were not accustom to seeing the commander so close to the fighting, so often. During the effort to rescue the Lost Battalion, the division commander was desperate to bring the mission to a successful conclusion. The darkest day yet for the Nisei would also be the General's darkest moment.

At dawn the 100th and 3d Battalion launched their attack, running directly into heavy resistance supported by enemy armor. It was the small Nisei infantrymen going head to head with multi-ton, steel fortresses of death. The brave soldiers never wavered. At eight in the morning General Dahlquist urged Colonel Singles to push his men onward. "There's a battalion about to die up there (in the mountains) and we've got to reach them." Before noon the General had arrived at the scene of the fighting with his young aide, Lieutenant Lewis. As Colonel Singles and the division commander viewed the terrain, an enemy machine gun some forty yards away opened fire. Twenty-seven year old Wells Lewis, the eldest son of the first American to receive the Nobel Prize for literature, Sinclair Lewis, fell dead. His blood splattered the uniform of his commanding general. It was a blow to the General from which he never fully recovered. Still, he remained in the field to issue orders and command the Nisei forward.

In the valleys, the Go For Broke Regiment's 232d Combat Engineers fought through the mud to shore up roadways with logs. Along the hillsides they cleared minefields and booby traps. Wounded were everywhere. James Okubo, the medic who had braved enemy fire the day before to rescue seventeen men continued his courageous efforts in the face of enemy fire to rescue eight more. His actions the previous day combined with his actions on the 29th to save a total of 25 wounded Nisei. He would survive to wear his Silver Star medal, but before his war would end there would be more lives to save.

Lieutenant Colonel Pursall of the 3d Battalion ordered Companies I and K to assault the high ground. His men were hesitant to move from the safety of their foxholes, knowing the assault would be deadly and useless. Standing in the open, bareheaded without a helmet, the Battalion commander raised his .45 Army Colt pistol and said, "Okay, boys, let's go." as he led the way forward in classic John Wayne style.

Second Lieutenant Edward Davis was the only officer left in company K. Slowly he rose to his feet as the Nisei around him watched in amazement. All knew the order to assault the enemy above them would be suicidal and were reluctant to move further. The lieutenant turned to Sergeant Kohashi and asked, not ordered, the NCO to follow him. Then something amazing happened. Sergeant Kohashi rose to his feet with a loud yell of desperation that reverberated across the hillside. It shook the Japanese-American soldiers to the soul, eliciting similar cries. As a unit, the Nisei leaped to their feet screaming "banzai" as they charged the Germans.

In his own sector, Private Barney Hajiro rose to his feet to lead his own assault. Next to him was a friend he had known since basic training, Takeyasu "Thomas" Onaga." As they moved forward young Hajiro watched in horror as the close friend who moments earlier had loaded his browning automatic rifle, fell dead to a hail of enemy bullets. The young private who had already twice demonstrated the highest degree of valor, could contain the torment of his soul no longer. With abandon he assaulted "suicide hill," yards ahead of the other men of his platoon, spewing the rounds his dead comrade had loaded in the BAR just moment earlier. Camouflage netting could not hide the enemy gunners from the fury of his assault, nor could the continuous stream of enemy machine gun fire turn back his determination. Private Barney Hajiro quickly knocked out two enemy gun emplacements and shot two snipers, allowing the rest of his unit to advance. Then enemy rounds slammed into Private Hajiro's left arm, rendering it useless.

The banzai charge on "suicide hill" consumed an hour. The Nisei suffered many casualties, but by 15:30 they had taken the hill. Those enemy soldiers who were wounded or otherwise unable to escape the hill, cowered in fear before the survivors of the onslaught. Never had they seen such courage, such fierce determination, and such sheer force of will power in the face of unbelievable odds.

These kinds of banzai charges, when looked upon in retrospect, further reveal the desperation to which the men of the 442d had been pushed. Pushed back on the line just one day after concluding their eight days of continuous combat to liberate Bruyères and Biffontaine, they suffered the physical maladies forced upon them by the cold, wet weather, and were driven beyond human endurance to accomplish what two previous regiments had been unable to do. After enduring such extreme conditions, their situation appeared hopeless. Many believed that relief would come only when they had freed the Lost Battalion or each man of the 442d Regiment had been destroyed. They were beaten beyond emotion, yet they could not help the emotions that rose up within their breast at the horrible slaughter around them.

Mr. George Sakato, a retired postal worker from Denver, Colorado looked back on October 29, 1944 fifty-six years later and summed the events up by saying, "Nowadays, they call it road rage." He should know, for he was there. His eyes still fill with tears whenever he is asked to recall the events of that day.

George Sakato

The men of Private Sakato's platoon from E Company knew their objective only as Hill 617. Sakato's citation tells how the men moved forward to take the hill, destroying two enemy positions. Private Sakato personally killed five enemy soldiers and captured four more. Then the enemy counter attacked.

Private Sakato and his buddy Saburo Tanamachi had been together since basic training. As the enemy launched their renewed assault, George turned to Saburo and told him to watch out for a machine gun. It was too late. The enemy rounds slammed into his friend, ripping flesh and spilling blood. As Saburo Tanamachi died in Sakato's arms, tears welled up within the young private's eyes. A rage began to boil deep within as he gently lowered his friend's lifeless body to the ground. Tears continuing to blur his vision he leaped to his feet, heedless of the enemy fire that tore into the brush around him, to launch his one-man assault on the Germans. Using an enemy rifle and pistol, he charged headlong into the counter-attack, killing twelve enemy soldiers, wounding two more and capturing four. Inspired by Private Sakato's brazen assault, his platoon followed, retaking the hill and capturing 34 prisoners. In all, Companies E and F killed 100 enemy and captured 41 in the taking of Hill 617.

It was the fifth day in the forest for the soldiers of the 442d as 3d Battalion led the way. The rain that had fallen virtually every day since October 15th began to turn to snow, altering conditions from bad to worse. Time was running out for the Lost Battalion and, equally important, the "cavalry" was running out of men to send to their rescue.

What remained of the 3d Battalion's I and K Companies joined with B and C Companies of the 100th. As a unit, they slogged their way down the ridge that led to the position of the Lost Battalion. To the left, the 2d Battalion was moving on the flank to dig out enemy soldiers and protect the Allied efforts on the ridge. Men of the 232d Engineers and the 522d Artillery were fighting as infantrymen; many replacing lost soldiers in the battered line companies. It would have been a beautiful display of complete teamwork by the Regiment, a tribute to their personal maturity since the squabbles months earlier when the 2d and 3d Battalion arrived in Italy, were it not for the sad loss of so many team members.

Leading the way was the decimated remains of I Company, which

Soldiers bow their heads in prayer as they remember their fallen comrades

soon ran into a roadblock manned by 50 Germans. K Company moved over to assist their badly outnumbered comrades, killing and routing the enemy and destroying the roadblock. Then, despite their fatigue, the Nisei moved on. Only two platoons remained in I Company which had been fully staffed at the beginning of the rescue mission, a company of 205 men: First Platoon consisted of six men, and Second Platoon had two. The highest-ranking officer of the eight-man company was an NCO, Sergeant Tak Senzaki. Shortly after 14:00, these men finally broke through to the Lost Battalion.

PFC Matt Sakumoto was the point man, the first friendly face the 211 survivors of the surrounded battalion had seen in a week. As the Nisei enlisted man walked past the first T-patcher he noticed the man's lips begin to quiver and his eyes fill with tears. He stared with relief and numbed shock at the miracle that had appeared out of the forest in the Vosges Mountains. It was an emotion charged moment of silence... what could either of them say to each other? Turning to the mud-blacken faces, tears streaming down the cheeks from sunken eyes, PFC Sakumoto could only say, "Want a smoke?"

Minutes later the rest of I Company broke through, and was joined shortly thereafter by K Company... or what remained of K Company, a mere seventeen men. In all the Nisei had lost 800 men in five days of battle to rescue 211 T-patchers of the 36th Infantry Battalion.

Sergeant Senzaki didn't allow his men time to reflect in their accomplishment, for the enemy was still nearby. He ordered his eight-man company to move on to take up defensive positions on the far side of the hill, protecting the men so many of his brothers had sacrificed to reach. Within an hour Lieutenant Blonder and his Lost Battalion were on their way down the hill, into the shelter of the waiting aid stations and the spotlight of a battery of newsmen. For those who survived, it was one of those experiences that stamps itself indelibly on the subconscious, never to be forgotten. For the 442d Regiment Combat Team, in a series of wartime accomplishments unprecedented in military history, it was a defining moment.

Pushed To The Limit: Fighting For Survival

"The best troops are called upon to do the hardest fighting. Whenever a general finds himself up against a tough proposition he sends for the best troops he has. In a critical situation he can't take chances with anything less than the best. A man who is being shot at daily has a hard time recognizing it as a compliment when, dead tired, bruised and battered, he is called upon to make one more effort to risk his life another time—but it is a compliment, nevertheless." (Colonel Sherwood Dixon, a War Department staffer in a letter to 442d RCT Chaplain Masao Yamada, 22 November 1944.)

THE RESCUE OF the Lost Battalion was indeed an historic moment for the 442d Regimental Combat Team. The *Presidential Unit Citation* (PUC) was awarded, individually, to each Battalion of the Go For Broke Regiment. The 100th recieved their second such award, added to the one received earlier in Italy and the 3d Battalion earning two in the twenty-one day campaign. A PUC was also awarded to the Regiment's 232d Combat Engineer Company.

Five men of the regiment were awarded the Distinguished Service Cross for their individual heroism during the incredible five-day ordeal to save the Lost Battalion. The rescued survivors of the Lost Battalion felt a debt of gratitude to the Nisei that still exists more than five decades later. Veterans are still moved to tears when they recount the joy of seeing the diminutive Japanese-American soldiers breaking through the forest to approach their position.

The rank and file among the Lost Battalion survivors launched a campaign to have all members of the 442d declared "honorary Texans." But for the sacrifice of the brave Nisei, Texas might have claimed a second Alamo. Such an honor was promised, but the promise was quickly forgotten. A few years after the war the men who owed their lives to the Nisei, now most of them civilians, would not let the forgotten promise fall by the wayside. Texas Governor John Connolly took the unprecedented step of issuing a proclamation declaring each and every member of the 442d Regimental Combat Team to be "Honorary Texans." Also, after the war, a painting was commissioned to depict the members of the 442d in action, battling through the Vosges to rescue the Lost Battalion. That painting has hung since at the Pentagon, a constant reminder of the incredible feat.

I Company Commander Captain James Wheatley submitted Private Barney Hajiro for both the Medal of Honor and the Victoria Cross. The wounded private, because of his nomination for his nation's highest award, was not allowed to rejoin his unit after recovering from his wounds. Instead, he was transferred to a segregated all-black unit. In 1948 he indeed received the Victoria Cross, the British equivalent of the United States Medal of Honor. His nomination for the Medal of Honor however, was downgraded to the Distinguished Service Cross. (That decision was eventually reversed, when his DSC was upgraded to the Medal of Honor over 50 years later.)

As quickly as the rescued members of the Lost Battalion were moved down the hill from the grasp of the enemy, the badly battered soldiers of the 442d pushed into the forest to secure the area. The Vosges was literally crawling with enemy soldiers including hundreds of fresh troops brought in to prevent the rescue that the Nisei had just miraculously accomplished. Sergeant Senzaki ordered his eight-man company to continue past the liberated Lost Battalion and into the forest on the far side of the ridge. A short time later the remains of Company K moved over to join them.

Upon learning that the Lost Battalion had been rescued, General Dahlquist wasted little time sending his thanks to his Nisei troops. His message came with new orders, "Take the next hill." Company K took the lead as the 3d Battalion continued forward in the offensive to secure the entire ridge. The day after the rescue, Company K was assigned a new officer to command the unit. Within 24 hours he was killed in action. By November 1st, the 3d Battalion had fewer than 200 men, less than a quarter of its full, authorized strength. Lieutenant Colonel Pursall told Regimental headquarters that if he didn't get more men he would have to withdraw and give the hill up to the Germans. Still, orders from Division headquarters were for the 442d, led by what remained of 2d Battalion, to not only hold but to push forward to completely remove the entrenched enemy from the ridge.

Companies I, K and L fought down the middle the ridge, with Companies F, G, and E covering the flanks. It was intense, bitter fighting that wore down soldiers already suffering the strain of too much misery, too many confrontations with the enemy, and too many friends killed.

On November 2d, when communicating via radio back to S-3, Lieutenant Colonel Pursall, was asked if there was anything that could be done for him, replied simply: "Relieve us!"

The only relief that arrived was the infusion of a few replacements

Painting by H. Charles McBarron still hangs at the Pentagon, depicts the historic rescue of the "Lost Battalion."

on November 3d. They were not infantrymen, but members of the 232d Engineers, assigned to replace the lost infantrymen of the 2d Battalion. Throughout the day they fought side by side with their comrades. As darkness fell on the night of November 3d, the Nisei had pushed the enemy to the forward areas of the ridge, withstood a strong counter-attack, and lost still more men. Despite the fact that finally the men of the 442d controlled the entire ridge, on the morning of November 4th General Dahlquist again ordered the 442d to attack and push the enemy from their positions on the forward slope of the ridge.

If the last week of October was a "shining star" in the crown of achievements of the 442d Regimental Combat Team, the first week of November was the blemish that dimmed a brilliant glow.

Historians will treat the manner in which General Dahlquist deployed and used his Nisei unit with mixed reviews. Among the veterans of the 442d there would be no doubt. They felt used, abused, squandered and pushed beyond any reasonable limits. Indeed years later after the war, Lieutenant Colonel Singles who had remained to pursue a career in the military, met General Dahlquist at a military ceremony. The former commander of the 442d dutifully (who is white), rendered a proper salute to the General who now sported four stars on his uniform. After returning the salute, General Dahlquist proffered his right hand saying, "Let bygones be bygones. It's all water under the bridge, isn't it?" Singles maintained his salute, ignoring the General's extended hand. Although he rendered proper military protocol, he could not forget what many considered the General's blatant waste of Japanese-American soldiers.

Despite the fact that historians may dispute General Dahlquist's performance, no one can dispute the performance of the soldiers of the 442d Regimental Combat Team during their darkest hours. Every advance meant fighting past the bodies of dead and dying comrades. Each soldier knew it was probably just a matter of time before they met a similar fate. You survived today, only to be lost tomorrow. The ridge was littered with the wounded, brave infantrymen as well as engineers forced to take up rifles and fight beside them. Among them moved the medics, struggling against hope to patch up broken bodies. There could be little satisfaction or sense of accomplishment in lives saved. A medic might patch up one soldier with minor wounds today, only to find him lying on the battlefield the next day with limbs shattered or missing, or dead. Indeed, 13 medics were themselves killed in action during the brief campaign in the Vosges Mountains.

On the morning of November 4th an impatient division commander asked when the 2d Battalion was going to push their way through the enemy along the forward edges of the ridge, and enter the villages below. He hung the "carrot" of hot showers in the houses below as an incentive. So thin were the ranks of the Nisei and so ever-present the power of the enemy, Lieutenant Colonel Pursall asked, "Who is going to hold the hill while we get down in those houses?" It was all too easy to remember how quickly Hill C had fallen back into enemy hands near Bruyères three weeks earlier after the 100th had fought so hard to take it. Colonel Pursall could not envision taking his men downhill to the farmhouses below, only to have the enemy retake the hill and use it to attack his men. Their showers could quickly turn into deadly showers. General Dahlquist refused to budge. The showers were simply an excuse. The goal was to keep the advance moving forward. Colonel Pursall followed orders, leading his men down the hill and directly into a minefield. Suddenly the enemy was everywhere, unleashing torrents of fire on the weary American soldiers.

Among the medics still trying to save lives was James Okubo, who had stayed in the field to treat the wounded for more than a week of continuous combat. Early in the effort to reach the Lost Battalion he had repeatedly risked his life to reach, treat and rescue wounded Nisei. Most notably he had been cited for a specific incident on October 28th, then again on October 29th. On November 4th as the Americans pushed deeper into the forest and ever closer to the German homeland, T/5 Okubo saw smoke rising from a Sherman tank that had been hit and destroyed by the Germans. Since the armor-protected tanks led the way for the infantrymen, the burning ruins were far forward of most friendly support, and dangerously close to the enemy. While small arms fire rained around him, he ran more than 75 yards into the fusillade to remove a wounded crewman from the burning tank, and carried him to safety. The commanding officers of the 442d recommended the brave medic for the Medal of Honor for his repeated efforts in the face of fierce enemy fire, to rescue and treat the wounded. They were told that, as a non-combatant medic, T/5 Okubo was not eligible for the Medal of Honor. Believing the Silver Star was the highest award for which the brave soldier was eligible; they submitted him for what is our nation's third highest combat decoration. After the war James Okubo returned home, eventually becoming a dentist in Detroit. When a review of the Asian Americans awarded the Distinguished Service Cross was undertaken in the 1990s to determine which should possibly be upgraded to the Medal of Honor, 21 were selected. To that group was added one additional hero. Under separate legislation James Okubo's Silver Star was upgraded, and the Medal of Honor was presented to his family. Dr. Okubo had died in an automobile accident 33 years earlier.

Meanwhile, there would be no showers for the weary Nisei. A determined enemy had halted their advance into the houses below the hill.

Though the incessant rain had turned into snow on the day of the Lost Battalion's rescue, the snow had been a wet, slushy snow that quickly melted. The first serious snowfall in the Vosges occurred on November 7th. Company I continued to press forward, though the entire company that had numbered 205 (even with replacements) at the beginning of the push, dwindled to only 34. Though each of the 442d's three regiments were assigned four infantry companies as well as a headquarters company, all three regiments were barely at the strength of a single company. The Purple Heart Battalion that numbered 1,432 men only a year earlier, now numbered only 239 infantrymen and twenty-one officers. The Second Battalion was largest, numbering 316 riflemen with seventeen officers. Not a single company in the Third Battalion had as many as 100 riflemen. The entire regiment had less than 800 soldiers.

The 2d Battalion's Company G had a total of 87 men and five officers. For three days the soldiers had fought their way across the ridge, unable to dislodge the well-fortified enemy. Each day men fell,

A Japanese-American unit (company F, 2nd Bn., 442nd Regiment - Combat Team) is holding a section of the Front Lines. November 1944

hidden mines and booby traps exploded, the enemy dropped more artillery, and even more soldiers suffered. On November 7th PFC Joe M. Nishimoto had had enough. The slightly built, mild mannered young infantryman from California turned into a one-man army. Though he was only a PFC, due to the loss of so many men, Joe Nishimoto was acting as an assistant squad leader. First he crawled through an enemy mine field to destroy one machine gun nest with a grenade.

Upon locating a second enemy position, he circled it to approach from the rear. His submachine gun spitting fire, he advanced on the startled Germans, killing one and wounding the second. Even when enemy soldiers tried to withdraw from the fearless soldiers onslaught, he refused to quit. He chased the enemy until he either destroyed them or forced them so far into the forest, they could no longer be a threat to his men. Before concluding his one-man campaign to win the war in the Vosges that day, he wiped out still another enemy machine gun, chasing the well entrenched enemy from their position. For his actions PFC Joe M. Nishomoto would be subsequently awarded the Distinguished Service Cross.

Joe Nishimoto

On November 9th, the 442d was finally ordered back. The soldiers had been in the field since October 15th with only the 1-2 day respite afforded them at Belmont on October 24-25, prior to their mission to rescue the Lost Battalion. When the Go For Broke Regiment had been attached to the 36th Infantry on October 13, 1944, the unit had been at full strength with 2,943 riflemen and officers. From the beginning of the first battles for Bruyères until the unit was relieved near La Houissiere more than three weeks later, 140 brave soldiers were killed in action, more than 1800 wounded, and forty-three were missing in action. Two days later, Veterans Day, General Dahlquist ordered the men of the 442d RCT to stand formation, during which he intended to recognize the men for their accomplishments. Afterwards the Chaplains would conduct a memorial service to honor those who had fallen in battle. As the general approached the small formation he was at first upset to see such a small gathering. "I want ALL your soldiers to stand for this formation," he told Lieutenant Colonel Miller of the 442d. The response: "This is all there is!"

Soon afterwards the 100th Battalion began preparing to move south. Meanwhile, on November 13th after less than four days rest, the 2d and 3d Battalions were again committed to combat. Compared to the hell the soldiers had just left, their return to the field for four days was a tolerable interruption of their recuperation period. It was not without casualties. On November 15th PFC Joe Nishimoto was killed in action, never to wear the DSC earned a week earlier, or to know it was upgraded fifty-six years later to the Medal of Honor. And, though not as severe as the previous weeks, there were still more casualties.

It would take months for the unit to rebuild to effective fighting strength. On November 19th General Dahlquist spoke of the Combat Team's five weeks with his division:

> *"The courage, steadfastness, and willingness of your officers and men were equal to any ever displayed by United States troops. Every man of the (36th Infantry) Division joins me in our best personal regards and good wishes to every member of your command, and we hope that we may be honored again by having you as a member of our Division."*

Color guards and color bearers of the Japanese-American 442d Combat Team, stand at attention, while their citations are read. They are standing on ground in the Bruyères area, France, where many of their comrades fell.

With those words General Dahlquist relinquished command the 442d Regimental Combat Team. What remained of the Regiment was to be attached to the 44th Anti-Aircraft Artillery Brigade with a mission to guard the Franco-Italian border. Compared to the hell the regiment left behind in the Vosges, it would be an almost five month "R & R" (rest and recuperation). There would still be casualties, more than sixty in the first three months in southern France. But as the Go For Broke Regiment left behind a Vosges campaign that had earned the unit an unprecedented fifth *Presidential Unit Citations* in 21 days, it was a welcomed reprieve.

The Champagne Campaign

"The sacrifice made by our comrades was great. We must not fail them in the fight that continues, in the fight that will be with us even when peace comes. Your task will be the harder and more arduous one, for it will extend over a longer time."
(Col. Virgil R. Miller, Commanding Officer, 442nd RCT at a memorial service held on May 6, 1945.)

IT WAS ALMOST Christmas and the sun warmed the Mediterranean and the hillsides along the French Riviera. From high above a small, sheltered bay a soldier from the 442d looked out across the distant range of the Alps, then back to the bright waters of the sea. The Go For Broke Regiment had finally been assigned some "pretty choice" duty.

From Switzerland to the north, the Alps ran down the western border of France, separating its boundaries from neighboring Italy. The 442d had been tasked with patrolling an eighteen-mile stretch from the coast northward. It was not without hazard; Nisei encountered enemy patrols from time to time. But it was certainly a whole different way to fight a war than what the weary soldiers had experienced in the Vosges. During the entire month of December, twenty members of the 442d were killed in action, which when compared to 140 KIAs in twenty-one days in the Vosges, was quite preferable.

The 100th Battalion had arrived first, snatching the prime job of patrolling near Nice on the French Riviera. Third Battalion had been assigned further north near Sospel, with Second Battalion going into the high mountains of the Alps. New replacements were arriving almost daily, as well as badly needed resupply.

The lookout chuckled to himself as he thought of the latter. Going into the Rhineland Campaign (the official title for the Vosges

Mountains actions), the 442d had no winter clothing. A requisition had been sent in for winter wear and other clothing for the Nisei. Finally some of the supplies had caught up to the quickly moving regiment: raincoats and clean underwear. When the men opened the boxes containing raincoats they found labels inside reading "WAC" (Women's Army Corps). Due the small stature of the Nisei as compared to other GIs, the Army Quartermasters had resorted to the women's' wear to find small enough raincoats for the men battling in the Vosges. When it is cold outside, you take what you can get, and the Nisei had bundled against the elements in the WAC raincoats without any sense of embarrassment. The clean underwear would have to wait. None of them would wear the panties that had arrived in boxes marked "shorts".

As the lookout chuckled to himself, he noticed a sudden flash of light on the waters of the bay. It was a reflection unlike the normal reflection from the sea. He shifted his position and peered more closely through the binoculars. It looked like a large whale might be floating on the surface. The lookout peered more closely through the binoculars and the "whale" began to take a more distinct shape. It was a small, two-man German submarine. Quickly he radioed his report back to headquarters, which dispatched a squad armed with 50 caliber machine guns and trench mortars.

The submarine seemed to be floundering in the bay, its crew struggling with mechanical difficulties, as the Nisei began a fifteen-minute attack on the submersible. In the face of the American attack, the two enemy soldiers guided their vessel to the sandy beach and surrendered. The submarine and its two submariners were handed over to the Navy. Less than a year later the story was related in a column in the *San Francisco Chronicle*. Reporter Robert O'Brien indicated "The 442d Regimental Combat Team is probably the only infantry unit in history to capture an enemy submarine."

It wasn't all work for the Go For Broke team. Passes were dispersed liberally. Certainly the brave soldiers of the 442d had earned some respite. It was a brief interlude that allowed them to rebuild the team, heal their bodies, and push horrible memories of the Vosges into their subconscious. Of course, the best sites in Southern France were restricted, but there has never been a war-weary GI that would let an "Off Limits" sign keep him from attractions like Monaco.

Amid the juggling act between mountain patrols and parties in the city, the Nisei even found time to become sympathetic to Southern France's innocent victims of World War II. As Christmas approached the men of 2d Battalion decorated a Christmas tree in the town square of one small French city, then invited the residents to join them in a holiday celebration. After a time of singing Christmas carols and sharing their own holiday spirit with the local citizens, the GIs started handing out Christmas gifts to the children. Each man had given a weeks rations to accumulate the candy and gifts they shared so freely with others.

Back in the United States, newspapers and magazines were beginning to relate the tale of the rescue of the Lost Battalion just weeks before. The 442d gained a national attention few military units ever achieved. Decorated veterans, wounded beyond further service were returning home and providing visual evidence of the courage and sacrifices of the Japanese-Americans of the 442d, as well as those serving in the Pacific in other units. Were it any other group of Americans, such high praise for the tremendous sacrifice of the Nisei would have a positive impact. But in some areas, such prejudice dies hard. In January, 1945 the American Legion Post in Hood River Oregon removed the names of sixteen Nisei servicemen, including one who had earned the Bronze Star Medal and another killed in action in the Philippines, from its honor roll of Veterans. And such acts of prejudice and hatred were not limited only to Oregon. Despite the sacrifice, many Americans refused to recognize the courage of our Japanese citizens.

Others however, began to deal with their irrational fears and prejudice. *Collier's* magazine blasted the act in Oregon calling it "tops in blind hatred." In the spring of 1944 Mary Masuda had returned to her home in Talbert, California from the relocation center in Gila. On May 4th a group of local men made a late night visit to terrorize her, warning that if she did not leave she might be physically injured. Frightened, she quickly departed. Then, in December the Army announced the award of the Distinguished Service Cross to Mary's brother Staff Sergeant Kazuo Masuda who had heroically sacrificed his life in Italy. Mary and her family were encouraged to return home to receive his award in a very public ceremony. The award was presented by General "Vinegar Joe" Stillwell who made his thoughts on such prejudice quickly clear:

> *"The Nisei bought an awful big hunk of America with their blood. You're damn right those Nisei boys have a place in American heart, now and forever. And I say we soldiers ought to form a pick-ax club to protect Japanese Americans who fought the war with us. Any time we see a barfly commando picking on these kids or discriminating against them, we ought to bang him over the head with a pick-ax. I'm willing to be a charter member. We cannot allow a single injustice to be done to the Nisei without defeating the purposes for which we fought."*
>
> General Joseph Stillwell

Back Southern France, Lieutenant Colonel James M. Hanley was more tactful but he still got his point across.

LTC Hanley was commander of the 2d Battalion, 442d Regimental Combat Team and a veteran of the fierce battles of the Vosges. As he relaxed with his men in southern France he had occasional opportunities to connect to his home via the receipt of his hometown newspaper. One day as he perused a copy of the *Mandan Daily Pioneer* from his home town of Mandan, North Dakota. He was both hurt and stunned by a comment in Editor Charles F. Pierce's column that read, "A squib in a paper makes the statement that there are some good Jap-Americans in this country but it didn't say where they are buried." On March 10th he scribbled off a reply that was printed three weeks later. It read:

> *Dear Charlie:*
>
> *Just received the Pioneer of Jan. 20 and noted the paragraph enclosed.*

Yes, Charlie, I know where there are some GOOD Japanese Americans—there are some 5000 of them in this unit. They are American soldiers—and I know where some of them are buried. I wish I could show you some of them, Charlie. I remember one Japanese American. He was walking ahead of me in a forest in France. A German shell took the right side of his face off. I recall another boy; an 88 had been trying to get us for some time—finally got him. When they carried him out on a stretcher the bloody meat from the middle of the thighs hung down over the end of the stretcher and dragged in the dirt—the bone parts were gone.

I recall a sergeant—a Japanese American if you will—who had his back blown in two—what was he doing? Why, he was only lying on top of an officer who had been wounded, to protect him from shell fragments during a barrage.

I recall one of my boys who stopped a German counterattack single-handed. He fired all his BAR ammunition, picked a German rifle, emptied that—used a German Luger pistol he had taken from a prisoner.

I wish I could tell you the number of Japanese Americans who have died in this unit alone.

I wish the boys in the "Lost Battalion" could tell you what they think of Japanese Americans.

I wish that all the troops we have fought beside could tell you what they know.

The marvel is, Charlie, that these boys fight at all—they are good soldiers in spite of the type of racial prejudice shown by your paragraph.

I know it makes a good joke—but it is the kind of joke that prejudice thrives upon. It shows a lack of faith in the American ideal. Our system is supposed to make good Americans out of anyone—it certainly has done it in the case of these boys.

You, the Hood River Legion post, Hearst (newspapers) and a few others make one wonder just what we are fighting for. I hope it isn't racial prejudice.

Come over here, Charlie, I'll show you where "some good Japanese Americans" are buried.

J. M. Hanley, HQ. 442d INF. APO 758

It was the dedication of the Nisei themselves that proved the loyalty and patriotism of our nation's Japanese-American citizens. Men like General Stillwell and Lieutenant Colonel Hanley did their best to point out this fact. Little by little the United States grew to truly appreciate the sacrifice of some of our nation's bravest sons. Colonel Hanley would have been proud to note that, though it would take 56 years, one day the last vestiges of that prejudice would disappear and one of the soldiers he had spoken of in his letter would live to see the President hang the Medal of Honor around his neck.

Even as Lieutenant Colonel Hanley was mailing his letter home, the period of rest was coming to an end for the men of the 442d Regimental Combat Team. In Italy, General Mark Clark wanted his Japanese-American unit to return to help finish the Italian campaign. They would return to some of the bitterest fighting yet. Fortunately for the Regiment's 522d Field Artillery, they would be spared the horrors of the climatic deadly campaign in Italy's Po Valley. Before the rest of the Regiment shipped out to Italy, the artillery unit was sent back up the Rhine Valley to join the 63d Division in their assault on the Siegfried Line.

From March 12 - 21, the unit gave fire support to the 63d. In the last week of March the Artillery Battalion crossed the Rhine River to provide support to the 4th Cavalry Reconnaissance Troop, then the famed 101st Airborne. On April 26, the regiment crossed the Danube with the 4th Infantry Division. During the period the unit supported seven different army divisions, fired more than 150,000 rounds on the enemy, and served in the post-war occupation army of Austria. It would be many months before the Nisei artillerymen would be reunited with their brothers. Before that reunion the rest of the 442d would make a final visit into a nightmare of combat on foreign shores.

For the men of the 522d Field Artillery, the pathway to victory in Europe led to an entirely different kind of nightmare, one perhaps even worse than combat.

Final Victory: Returning to Italy

ON MARCH 28, 1945 the 100th/442d Regimental Combat Team departed France to return to Italy. The unit had been brought back to regimental strength through the arrival of replacements throughout the winter. For the men who had been with the team since the early days and had survived the Vosges, upon arriving near Pisa, it was almost as if time had stood still during the team's absence. Very little had changed.

In the previous campaign the 100th/442d had joined the Fifth Army in the bitter battle to secure the western coast of Italy, digging out the well-fortified enemy emplacements on the western ridges of the high Appenine Mountains. From the 100th Infantry Battalion's landing at Salerno on September 26, 1943, to the movement of the reunited Combat Team into France a year later, the Nisei had fought their way past Rome to secure the area from Pisa to Florence south of the Arno River. Prior to their departure for the campaign in the Vosges, the team had crossed the Arno River to battle German soldiers all along the area south of the Gothic Line. Upon their return, the Go For Broke Regiment found the Allied advance on the western coast of northern Italy still stalled before the formidable Gothic Line. Throughout the winter the enemy had built up their forces, reinforced their positions, and strengthened their hold in the high mountains.

The Allied campaign to push the Germans out of Italy had been a veritable coalition of wide national and ethnic diversity. The British Eighth Army had battled along the eastern slopes of the Apennines, the Canadians had liberated Ravenna and a New Zealand unit had battled its way into Senio. Polish soldiers had fought valiantly throughout the campaign, most notably in the struggle to take Monte Cassino, an effort that almost wiped out an entire Polish battalion. French Moroccan Goums became renown for their fierce fighting, the 8th Indian Division supported the United States Fifth Army, and the Brazilian Corps of 25,000 soldiers entered the battle for Italy in August 1944. The American Fifth Army also included the 92d Division, the all-black American Army unit.

The battle for northern Italy had continued for these Allies through the winter of 1944-45. While the 442d had fought valiantly in the Vosges, they assumed their border patrols in Southern France. Late in 1944 General Mark Clark was appointed to command the 15th Army Group and command of the Fifth Army had fallen to General Lucian Truscott. While the advance had stalled along the Gothic Line, General Clark began developing a plan to crush enemy resistance by ordering the Fifth Army in a bold frontal assault on the Gothic Line while simultaneously moving the Eight Army westward from Bologna to trap the fleeing enemy and crush them near the Po River.

General Mark W. Clark. 5th Army Group, welcomes men of the 442nd RCT and of the 100th Bn., now under under his command. Gen. Clark formerly commanded them during their first Italian campaign, but they were transferred to the 34th Division in France. General Clark asked if they liked Italy better than France, most of the men gave Gen. Clark a hearty "no!"

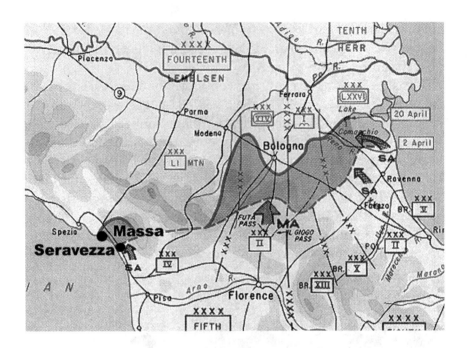

Meanwhile, German Field Marshall Kesselring swiftly moved four divisions westward to bouy up his heavy fortifications north and west of the Gothic Line. Using more than 15,000 slave-laborers, the Germans created more than 2,000 well-fortified machine gun nests, observation posts, and fighting positions to repel any attempt to breach the Gothic Line.

The early months of 1945 provided a brief respite for the weary Allied troops, as clandestine meetings were held at the highest military levels in neighboring Switzerland. There were rumors of a German surrender, and in March top aides to both the Allied and Axis forces met in the Sunrise negotiations. Even as it seemed the war might end without further bloodshed to breach the Gothic Line, General Mark Clark continued to plan his offensive as an alternative. To spearhead the drive along the western coast, General Clark turned to the soldiers that had successfully overcome every obstacle they had been assigned in Italy. On March 28th, the 442d Regimental Combat Team left France to take up positions near Pisa, an area they had left six months earlier. Their redeployment below the Gothic line was a closely guarded military secret. When the last hopes of a negotiated surrender by the Germans fell through on April 1st, General Clark launched his offensive.

On the night of April 1, British commandos along the eastern coast began raids near Lake Comacchio bordering the Adriatic. The move on the eastern side of the Gothic line drew swift attention to the flank, allowing the Eight Army to prepare for their assault across the Senio River that ran eastward from the Apennines to the Adriatic. While the Eighth Army was assaulting the right side of the Gothic Line, the Fifth Army was preparing to assault on the left.

The offensive on the west side of the Gothic Line from Florence to Pisa would be spearheaded by the newly arrived 442d Regimental Combat Team, now assigned to the all-black 92d Infantry Division. On April 3d the Anti-Tank Company divided its four platoons among the RCT's three Battalions, two of the platoons being assigned to the 3d Battalion. The anti-tank units would provide two primary support roles, carrying badly needed ammunition and supplies *in* to the soldiers as they attacked the Gothic Line. They were also assigned to carry *out* the bodies of the dead and wounded that would surely follow the attack.

Rising up from the Ligurian Sea, a series of high mountains spread inland to provide a natural barrier to the advance northward towards Massa. They also provided rugged concealment for the well-entrenched enemy. Each mountaintop led to the next, each higher than the one before. First were Georgia, then Florida, Ohio 1, Ohio 2, Ohio 3, Mount Cerreta and Mount Folgorita. Just inland from Massa were three more major mountaintops critical to control of the area, Mount Belvedere, Mount Carchio, and the dominant inland peak of the 3000-foot high Mount Altissimo. Breaking through the Gothic Line would require taking each mountain in turn, all the while under fire from the large coastal guns at La Spezia.

As darkness fell on April 3rd the 100th Battalion was moving quietly into the small town of Vallechio below the high tops of Georgia and Florida. Third Battalion moved by truck to the flank, using the cover of the dark night to silently traverse up the valley facing Azzano to the east of Mount Cerreta. Men slipped and fell beneath backpacks laden with supplies and ammunition as the Nisei forged through the darkness, never breaking silence. The following day the two battalions, still maintaining strict silence, positioned themselves for the first day of the renewed offensive. The Purple Heart Battalion relieved the 371st Infantry at Florida, the Third Battalion positioning itself near Mount Folgorita and Mount Carchio. As the calendar turned to the opening day of April 5, the Germans still had no idea that the Japanese-American soldiers they had come to fear a year before, now lay hidden below their mountaintop fortifications. Before daylight dawned, they would be awakened to the sudden realization that the Go For Broke Regiment was back in Italy, ready to break through their venerable Gothic Line and put an end to the stalemate that had gone on for months. At 0500 the order was given to the Nisei of the Purple Heart Battalion to attack. The Gothic Line was about to be Broke

On April 5, PFC Sadao Munemori watched from his place of concealment as the first American artillery rounds began to rain down on Georgia Hill. He knew the "vacation" was over. The young soldier had joined the Purple Heart Battalion as a replacement at Anzio nearly a year before. After fighting through Italy, then the Vosges, the 22-year old Nisei had aged far beyond his years. Life had already given the young man a hefty burden to bear.

Sadao had been born in Los Angeles shortly after his parents emigrated from Japan, and the family quickly became Americanized. Sadao and his two brothers and sisters had heard stories of Japan from their parents, who frequently reminded their children how fortunate they were to be raised in the United States with its freedom and liberty. Then, when Sadao was only 18 years old, his father had died leaving the young man to assume the responsibilities for the Munemori household. Young Sadao

Sadao Munemori

had worked hard as an auto mechanic in his native Los Angeles to support the family. The following year Pearl Harbor was attacked. Outraged, young Sadao Munemori tried to enlist in the Army. He was rejected because of his parentage. Then, to further darken the young American's future, the country his parents had always praised for its freedoms, took away the liberty of the Munemori family. The family lost almost everything, allowed only to carry a few items to their new "home" at the Manzinar relocation camp. When finally the success of the 100th Infantry Battalion convinced the War Department to seek volunteers for an all Japanese-American military unit, Sadao quickly volunteered.

PFC Munemori watched for ten minutes as the heavy American artillery rounds pounded Georgia Hill, the thunder of their explosive force reverberating through the valley below. In their fortified positions, the enemy took cover from the fierce shelling. At 0500 the artillery fire began to cease. As the enemy tried to regroup they were faced with a sight they had not expected to see. Hundreds of Japanese-American soldiers were making a frontal assault on the hilltop near Seravezza that the Germans had held for months. The Go For Broke Regiment had returned to Italy, and their presence was no longer a secret.

Quickly the enemy began to recover from the shelling to rain machine gun fire on the advancing Nisei, interspersed with occasional grenades. As Company A attacked, PFC Munemori watched his squad leader fall, wounded by a German grenade. The young Munemori took control of the squad, leading them through the enemy's protective minefield to within 30 yards of the first machine gun nest. Then the Germans turned their machine guns on the advancing squad. Quickly the men, many of them replacements tasting combat for the first time, dived for the protection of the craters the earlier artillery barrage had created on the hilltop. Pressing their bodies firmly into the dirt, the continuous fire from two enemy gun emplacements had them pinned down and at the mercy of the enemy.

Checking his own supply of ordinance, PFC Munemori grabbed grenades from a couple of his men, arming himself for a one-man assault. Moving within 15 yards of the enemy as lethal missiles rained around him, the 22-year old combat veteran threw his first grenade, then another, and another. In all, the brave Nisei managed to lob six grenades, destroying both enemy machine gun nests.

With the immediate threat destroyed, the PFC began to work his way back to his squad of men huddled in their shell holes. Other machine gun nests opened fire as he moved back, and enemy soldiers began throwing grenades. As Munemori reached his men he felt something hard slam into his helmet, then it fell to the ground inside the shell hole where two of his soldiers waited. Quickly Munemori dove on top of the grenade, covering it with his body as it detonated. Beside him, two soldiers survived because of the young hero's sacrifice.

All along the slopes of Georgia, other soldiers of the Purple Heart Battalion pressed the assault. Half an hour later the shooting began to die down, and the enemy was being routed. In half an hour the Purple Heart Battalion had taken Georgia Hill, the opening steps in the month-long campaign to end the war in Italy.

To the northeast, 3rd Battalion had spent the previous night climbing towards Mount Folgorita. There would be no rest, for after an all-night hike, Company L launched the attack on its objectives at at 0600. The enemy alerted the coastal batteries at La Spezia and German artillery and mortars began to create a curtain between the Nisei and the well-fortified Germans. Heedless of the explosions that ripped the mountainside, the Nisei pressed forward, often engaging the enemy in hand-to-hand combat. Meanwhile Company K, reinforced by an M Company mortar platoon, began a bold, daylight climb towards the crest of Mount Folgorita. From their high vantage point on Mount Altissimo, the enemy rained effective mortar fire on the brave Nisei. Seventeen young Nisei were killed, and eighty-three were wounded. Still the company pressed their attack, destroying one enemy stronghold after another.

As the exhausted, battle-weary Nisei settled in for the night, they knew that some of the worst was yet to come. That very night the Germans launched a counter-attack on the Purple Heart Battalion

*Light tanks mounted with 75 mm Howitzer, fire in support of
the 442nd RCT near Seravezza*

in a strong effort to retake their strategic positions. Despite the fact that the men had been nearly two days without sleep, they fought back valiantly and repulsed the enemy.

The attack of the combat team had caught the Germans totally unprepared. The secret arrival of the Nisei had been well guarded. The sudden appearance of the Japanese-American unit had stunned the enemy, both by its presence on the Gothic Line as well as by the ferocity of its fighting men. In the first day the Germans lost 30 men killed in action, even more wounded or captured. Perhaps more important, they had lost a dozen well-fortified bunkers, 17 machine guns, and three big 75mm howitzers.

In the darkness the Nisei pondered their own losses as well, 100 casualties for Company K alone. Stories of the heroism of the day also passed among the exhausted soldiers, giving them new resolve. Stories like that of PFC Henry Arao who had single-handedly knocked out two enemy machine gun nests, one after crawling through a minefield. And the story of the young PFC from Los Angeles who lost everything in an American relocation camp to come to Italy and fight for the nation that had once disowned him, ultimately giving his own life to save the lives of his men. The story of Sadao Munemori could not be ignored. If indeed there was still racial prejudice in the American military that prevented the Japanese-American soldiers from receiving their nation's highest award for military valor, that prejudice was silenced by Munemori's valiant spirit. On April 7, 1947, almost two years to the day, a quiet but dignified ceremony was held to honor an American hero. On that day Sadao Munemori's mother accepted his Medal of Honor. For 56 years it would remain the only Medal of Honor awarded to a Japanese-American for heroism in World War II. (Sadao Munemori's Medal of Honor is now on public display at the Smithsonian in Washington, D.C.

With the dawn of April 6th the soldiers of the 442d continued to press the attack. By mid-day the Nisei had secured the area all the way from Georgia to Mount Folgorita. Only Ohio 1, 2 and 3 remained with any measured resistance, much of the enemy now cut off from the rest of their command. Throughout the day American artillery pounded the last defenders, effectively nullifying their impact on the advance through the mountains.

Meanwhile, Company L assaulted and took control of Mount Cerreta and Company F and Company I took control of Mount Carchio in the shadow of Mount Belvedere and Mount Altissimo. The latter were the only remaining major enemy positions between the Nisei and a complete breach of the Gothic Line.

Company F had been able to lend their assistance to 3d Battalion's I Company at Mount Cerreta because the 2d Battalion was already in the area. While the fighting had raged on the ridgelines from Georgia to Mount Folgorita, the Second Battalion had been positioning itself for the assault on the all-important Mount Belvedere overlooking Massa and the Frigido River. Limited action on April 6th gave way to the full-scale assault on April 7th. It would culminate two days of combat to roust the crack Kesselring Machine Gun Battalion and the effort to break open the Po Valley campaign. In three days the 442d Regimental Combat Team would end a stalemate that had existed for the entire six months they had been gone.

Mount Belvedere was the one remaining major obstacle facing the advance of the 442d, and 2nd Battalion attacked from the heights of Mount Folgorita with a vengeance. As seemed to be the *modus operandi* for the entire effort to move up the coastline, the Nisei had spent the previous night hiking up mountain trails to get into position, and then already exhausted and without sleep, they attacked at dawn. One unfamiliar with the terrain might envision a series of individual mountains among the dominant peaks stretching along the Gothic Line. In actuality, it was more a series of peaks along a continuous ridge line, each separated by a low-lying saddle. The approaches varied from dense forests to dangerous open expanses of loose shale. Embedded on all approaches were the hidden, well-fortified machine gun nests of the Kesselring Battalion.

Darting from boulder to boulder, the 2nd Battalion advanced on the Germans entrenched on Mount Belvedere. Mortar fire began to fall among the ranks of the Nisei as the enemy struggled to hold their last bastion in the chain of mountains that sheltered Massa and the Frigido River. Company F was moving forward when three enemy emplacements opened up on one of its platoons in a deadly crossfire that halted the advance and sent the men seeking cover. Huddled among the rocks, the scattered Nisei were at the mercy of the enemy fire, unable to move in any direction. Unless something dramatic happened soon, the enemy would be able to drop accurate mortar fire on the embattled platoon while the machine guns kept them pinned in position.

Technical Sergeant Yukio Okutsu watched the deadly fire criss-cross the hillside, lethal missiles of hot lead reaching out to kill his men. Slowly he began to crawl towards the first enemy position, moving within 30 yards. Then he rose up, throwing two grenades. The enemy gun fell silent, and the men who had manned were dead. Sergeant Okutsu moved on. Locating the position of the second gun, he darted from rock to rock, and then hugged the barren ground to crawl from one vantage point to the next. Again he rose up to throw a well-aimed grenade in the direction of the enemy. The second position fell silent, two of its gunners lay wounded. The remaining enemy quickly

surrendered. A third position continued to
rain a torrent of death on the Nisei. Bullets
ricocheted off the hard shale of the hillside
as Sergeant Okutsu continued his one-man
assault. His men watched his onslaught in
amazement, rendering what cover fire they
could. Suddenly the brave sergeant staggered from the impact of a hard blow to the
head. As Okutsu staggered, his men could
hear the sound of the impact on his helmet.
Fortunately, the round was deflected by the
steel pot and he recovered quickly. Sergeant

Yukio Okutsu

Okutsu rushed the enemy position with his submachine gun spitting
fire. Under the unrelenting charge, the enemy withdrew. Sergeant
Okutsu's men were spared, able to rise up and move forward.

The Nisei of the 2d Battalion spent the day going head-to-head with
the fortified positions of some of Germany's finest machine gunners.
In the end, it was the brave American soldiers who prevailed. The
Kesselring Machine Gun Battalion was, for all practical purposes,
not only nullified... but destroyed.

The secret return of the 442d Regimental Combat Team was certainly no longer a secret; the valiant unit had made an astonishingly
quick and successful assault on the Gothic Line, and broken it. The
two-day offensive left the German forces stunned, survivors pulling
back in a hasty and poorly organized withdrawal. The April 8th issue
of *Stars and Stripes* told the story under a headline that read:

> *The 45th's attack spearheaded by 442 Nisei Regiment: "They (the
> 442d) remained within carefully guarded bivouac areas until
> last Wednesday. Then under cover of darkness, they moved into
> the line, and hid within mountain villages until the attack was
> launched. German prisoners said they had been caught completely
> by surprise."*
>
> Stars And Stripes

So swiftly had the Nisei taken their objectives, it was often hard for the supply line behind them to keep up with the advancing soldiers on the front line. While 2d Battalion had been assaulting Mount Belvedere the previous day, 3d Battalion's Company K had been moving so swiftly they had actually moved beyond their initial enemy-held objective. Turning back, they approached their assigned position from the rear, catching the enemy unprepared and quickly capturing 20 of them.

The battle was still far from over. Pockets of resistance still confronted the advancing Nisei in the days that followed. But the Allies now controlled Highway 1 along Italy's western coastline. Needed supplies flowed quickly and freely northward from Pisa to Massa. The soldiers of the 442d pressed their advantage, liberating the Italian towns at a rate of two or three a day. Within three days of the opening assault they had taken the high ground around Massa, opened Highway 1 from Pisa to Massa, and continued to push the enemy off their vaunted Gothic Line. For the following five days the team continued to fight, taking the towns of Montignoso, Altagnana and Pariana. The latter was a small village to which the survivors of the Kesselring Machine Gun Battalion had withdrawn. All day and into the night, 2d Battalion's E and F Companies took the battle to the 150 survivors of the infamous German battalion. By April 10th, of the 150 enemy trapped in the village, 65 were killed and 62 were captured. Twelve enemy mortars and eight enemy machine guns were taken as well in the fierce fighting.

Without a pause, the 442d pushed onward past Massa and towards Carrara, half a mile past the Frigido River. Carrera fell quickly as the enemy retreat turned into a rout. The following day the towns of Gragnana and Sorgnano were taken, almost without a shot. By Thursday, April the twelfth, Highway 1 was opened from Massa to Carrara, and it seemed nothing would stop the invincible Nisei. But that was the day before.

A week later, on Friday the 13th, Second Battalion had moved five miles north of Carrara, passing by the towns of Gragnana and

Castelpoggio and chasing the fleeing enemy. Unknown to the Nisei, from high atop Mount Pizzacuto, the Germans could plainly view the advance of the American Soldiers below. Just as Second Battalion reached the base of the mountain the German gunners opened fire. The battalion was quickly pinned down, as was the Purple Heart Battalion slightly a mile behind them. The advance halted and casualties began to mount. The enemy had been retreating in disarray, but it became quickly apparent that the war in Italy wasn't over yet.

The heavy enemy coastal guns at La Spezia pounded both American battalions, also dropping heavy artillery on 3d Battalion, which was being held in reserve at Carrara. For the Americans there was no friendly heavy fire support. So quickly had the Go For Broke Regiment advanced, their supporting artillery could not keep up

Traffic moves over by-pass and crosses the Frigido River on the outskirts of Massa. The by-pass was built by an engineering company of the 442nd RCT

with them. Under cover of darkness that night, Company B slipped quietly into Castelpoggia to support the 2d Battalion's command group. Meanwhile, also during the night, the Allied artillery moved its big guns forward to lend support.

As dawn broke the skies on April 14th, the Germans sent a battalion to attack Castelpoggia. They were caught unprepared by the developments of the dark hours of the previous night. In the bitter fighting that followed, the enemy was thrown back with many casualties. The Nisei suffered five of their own comrades killed in action, five more wounded, but the Americans had held.

In the week that followed the Allied advance continued at a furious pace. On April 17th the Germans destroyed their railroad guns at La Spezia, pulling back to concentrate their forces in and around Aulla in the Po Valley. For three days the enemy continued to destroy their fortifications to keep them from falling to the Allies, while pulling all their manpower into a tight "last ditch defense" of Aulla.

To take Aulla the Nisei battled their way over Mount Pizzaculo and Mount Grugola stretching along the coast from Castelpoggio to Aulla. Along the way they entered the small town of San Terenzo. From there the attacks would be launched to take Aulla, Task Force Fukuda (consisting of Companies B and F) sweeping in from the coast, the 100th and 3d Battalions attacking from the inland side. In their path loomed the towering heights of Mount Nebbione southeast of Aulla, the last high ground to protect the Germans fighting for survival in Italy.

On April 19th, 2nd and 3d Battalions assaulted Mount Nebbione. After a day of fierce fighting, the enemy held and the Nisei pulled back to recover and plan for a renewed effort. On their flank the 100th was lending support by taking the town of Marciaso and Posterla. Next in line for the Purple Heart Battalion was Colle Musatello. The order to attack came early on the evening of April 20th.

Lieutenant Daniel Inouye positioned his rifle team for the assault in the early morning darkness. With the first rays of sunshine, his rifle platoon would join two others in the assault on the heavily defended ridge that was Colle Musatello. Lieutenant Inouye and his men had faced far too many ridges like this in the previous weeks, but today things were different. The 20-year old Nisei officer had an eerie feeling something bad was about to happen.

Daniel Inouye had trained with the 442d at Camp Shelby, shipped out with the team to Europe, and landed with it nearly a year earlier at Naples. Promoted enroute to buck sergeant, he was transferred to the 100th Infantry Battalion as a replacement, and had fought through the first drive north to the Arno River. He had survived war in the Vosges, missing the Rescue of the Lost Battalion only because he had been pulled back to headquarters for a field promotion to lieutenant. By the time he got back to his men, the rescue was completed. His platoon had been cut in half by the horrible fighting, and Lieutenant Inouye began the arduous task of rebuilding his part of the Go For Broke team.

Lieutenant Inouye had seen nine months of combat, and had served with pride and honor, remembering the words of his father the day he had left to begin training with the 442d:

"Son, you know what 'on' means?"

"Yes, father."

"The Inouyes have a great 'on' for

Daniel Inouye

America. It has been good to us. And now it is you who must try to return the goodness. You are my first son, and you are very precious to your mother and to me, but you must do what must be done. If it is necessary, you must be ready to... to..."

"I know, Papa. I understand."

"Son, Do no bring dishonor on our name."

As the first rays of sunlight began breaking through the morning skies, Lieutenant Inouye still couldn't shake his uneasy feeling. He

("On" is a Japanese colloquialism, very deep in the Japanese culture. It requires that when one man is aided by another, he incurs a debt that is never canceled, one that must be repaid at every opportunity.) From Daniel Inouye's Autobiography

put his hand to the breast pocket of his uniform again, feeling nothing. And that was the problem. Throughout nine months of combat, he had always felt the hard shape of two silver dollars in that pocket. One was cracked, the other bent... but the enemy bullet that had damaged the two coins was halted and had left only a dark bruise on the flesh over his heart. Had it not been for the two coins, Lieutenant Inouye would have been killed in the battlefields of France. From the moment the two silver dollars saved his life, the Nisei officer had carried them in the same pocket through every campaign, through every battle. The previous day, somehow, they had fallen out. Well into the night he had searched in vain to find them. Now, with the order to attack, their absence sent a foreboding sense of disaster to his young mind.

Realizing how irrational his regard was for the two "lucky charms," Lieutenant Inouye prepared his men for the assault. Two other rifle platoons would attack Colle Musatello from the front, Lieutenant Inouye's 3d platoon moving in on the left flank. At the first sounds of gunfire from the other two platoons, Inouye led his own men forward.

At first it seemed the feelings of impending disaster had been foolish. Lieutenant Inouye skillfully led his men forward and, despite heavy opposition, quickly overcame every enemy position. Third platoon met and quickly defeated an enemy patrol, captured a mortar position, and moved within 40 yards of the main defensive force of the Germans on Colle Musatello. So well had the attack been coordinated by third platoon, it was in position to attack the main fortifications while first and second platoons were still struggling to make their way through enemy defenses further down the ridge. Almost within grenade range of the enemy, Lieutenant Inouye had to make a decision. Either his men could take shelter and wait for the other two platoons to catch up or they could attack.

Lieutenant Inouye didn't *order* his men forward. He *led* them forward. Rising, the platoon began their assault on the last German stronghold, and Lieutenant Inouye was well out in front of them. Three enemy machine guns began spitting at the advancing Nisei, pressing them to take cover. Alone in advance of his men, Lieutenant Inouye took a grenade from his belt and rose up to throw it. As he did, he felt a powerful blow to his side. Ignoring the pain, he counted three seconds and lobbed the grenade. As the enemy pulled back from their destroyed position, Lieutenant Inouye stood his ground to cut them down, all the while motioning his men forward. When finally they reached Inouye's position, one of them said, "My God, Dan, you're bleeding! Get down and I'll get an aid man." It was only then that the young officer realized he had been shot in the side as he had risen up to throw his grenade.

The other two enemy gun positions continued to fire on the Nisei platoon. Ignoring his pain, Lieutenant Inouye forced his body forward, rushing towards the second enemy position. Moments before his legs collapsed from under him, he managed to close in on the second position and throw two more grenades. The second enemy gun fell silent, even as the broken body of Dan Inouye collapsed to the ground.

"Go For Broke," yelled one of the soldiers of Inouye's platoon as the brave Nisei charged headlong into the third enemy machine gun. A curtain of enemy fire met them. Heedless of the danger, they pressed forward, struggling to maintain consciousness. Their wounded Lieutenant watched their display of raw courage with great pride and admiration. But raw courage could not shield flesh and blood from the ravages of the hot lead rained on their platoon. The attack faltered, the survivors of Inouye's third platoon were forced to pull back and seek cover.

The valiant charge had given the wounded officer more than just an opportunity to observe his men in action. Their assault had monopolized the attention of the enemy in the last machine gun nest. Lieutenant Inouye had used the diversion to great advantage, dragging himself unseen along the enemy flank. Even as the attack faltered, Lieutenant Inouye was close enough. He forced his body, weakened by loss of blood, to respond beyond its limits. He pulled the pin on his last grenade, and then stood to release the spoon and throw it. As he rose, one of the enemy spotted him and quickly fired a rifle grenade at the lone Nisei. There was a horrible explosion and a searing pain in the young lieutenant's arm. When Inouye looked down, his arm was destroyed, hanging in place by only a few string-like tendons. The grenade was still clutched to his nearly detached hand that could no longer respond to impulses from the brain.

The men of third platoon were horror-struck, rising up to rush to the aid of their commander. "Get back!" Inouye screamed at them. With his one good hand he pried the grenade from the frozen fingers of his useless right and threw it at the enemy. Then, stumbling to his feet and firing his tommy-gun left handed, he continued to advance through the smoke and dust of its explosion to kill all but one of the enemy. The last survivor sent a burst of fire in the direction of the brave lieutenant, advancing fearlessly while what remained of his mangled arm flopped uselessly at his right side. One round hit Lieutenant Inouye in the right leg, halting his advance and sending him rolling down the hillside.

Quickly the men of third platoon rushed to the side of their leader's body. He had been shot in the stomach, the right leg, and his right arm had been destroyed beyond repair. As they reached his side, the young officer gritted his teeth through the pain and ordered, "Get back up that hill! Nobody called off the war." They did, and inspired by their brave lieutenant, they took their position.

On the same day that Lieutenant Inouye had lost his two silver dollars, and as Company E was preparing for their assault on Colle Musatello, 3d Battalion had moved within ten miles of Aulla. Company K had attacked along the hillsides above Tendola when enemy machine gun fire halted the advance and left the slopes littered with the bodies of wounded Nisei. Private Joe Hayashi had moved his men within 75 yards of the enemy before they fell to the enemy fire. Despite the heavy enemy fire, Private Hayashi dragged the bodies of his wounded friends downhill and out of harm's way. Then he returned to the center of com-

Joe Hayashi

bat, boldly advancing alone and in full view of the enemy, to direct and adjust supporting mortar fire. When the bombardment began to die down, Private Hayashi took command of what remained of his platoon and led them forward to capture the hilltop. Because of Hayashi's courage in standing openly in the field of battle to direct the fire of the mortar crews, three machine gun nests had been destroyed and twenty-seven enemy soldiers killed.

Throughout the remainder of the April 20th, and into the following day, while Lieutenant Inouye and the 100th Battalion had battled for control of the San Terenzo area, 3rd Battalion fought to claim each of the hillsides above Tendola. The attack on Tendola itself commenced on April 22nd.

Private Hayashi's squad was assigned to take a steep hillside above Tendola, a mission not unlike the one two days earlier when the brave infantryman had so distinguished himself. On this day Private Hayashi moved his squad up the steep, terraced hillside to within 100 yards of the enemy. As the Germans machine guns opened fire on the Nisei with their heavy machine guns, Private Hayashi crawled forward alone until he was close enough to destroy the enemy position with a well-placed grenade. While pursuing the enemy, Hayashi noticed other elements of his platoon being raked by fire from four additional enemy positions. Hayashi lobbed a grenade at the closestone, destroying it. He then crawled to the right flank of another, killing four of the enemy gunners and forcing the remaining enemy to abandon the position. As he attempted to pursue the fleeing enemy soldiers, a burst of machine pistol fire erupted his way. Private Hayashi would become one of the last casualties of the war for the 442nd. When his posthumous award of the Distinguished Service Cross was upgraded to the Medal of Honor fifty-six years later, his would become the last Medal of Honor action by a member of the 442nd Regimental Combat Team, and the last such action by any U.S. Army infantryman on the fields of battle in Europe during World War II.

San Terenzo fell on April 23rd, second battalion killing forty enemy and capturing 135. Meanwhile third battalion finally took Mount

Nebbione and Mount Carbolo, and Major Mitsuyoshi Fukuda led his "Task Force Fukuda" to control the important road junction that was the German lifeline to Aulla. Two days later when Aulla fell with second battalion and Task Force Fukuda advanced into the town in a pincer movement that cut off all hope for the enemy.

In the days that followed, 2d Battalion moved into Alessandra and Asti, the 100th Battalion took Busalla, and 3d Battalion moved in to control Genoa after it had fallen to the Italian Partisans. The Fifth and Eighth Armies continued their advance into the Po Valley where, on April 24-25 Army Air Force First Lieutenant Raymond Knight received the last Medal of Honor of WWII's European theater of operations for his low-level strafing missions over the Po Valley. He was killed in action on the 25th.

On May 2, 1945 the war ended in Italy. On May 6th the Go For Broke Regiment held a memorial service at Novi Liguria near Genoa for its fallen comrades. In all, the regiment had suffered nearly 700 killed in action, sixty-seven missing in action, and nearly 10,000 wounded in action. Three days after the memorial service, Germany surrendered. On May 9, 1945 World War II ended in Europe.

War In The Pacific: MIS and the Nisei

"Before World War II, I entertained some doubt as to the loyalty of American citizens of Japanese ancestry in the event of war with Japan. From my observations during World War II, I no longer have that doubt."

Admiral Chester W. Nimitz.

BEN AND FRED Kuroki grew up in the small town of Hershey, Nebraska....population less than 500. When Pearl Harbor was attacked, their father called a family conference and urged his sons to enlist in the Army. "America is your country," he told the boys. On December 10th, three days after the opening volley of World War II, the two young Japanese-Americans joined the line of young men at recruiting headquarters in Grand Island, Nebraska. Both were refused enlistment because they were "Japs." Hurt and discouraged, the two young patriots refused to give in to the prejudice that faced them. Two months later they drove to North Platte, where they were finally accepted.

Both young men faced tremendous prejudice as they trained with all white volunteers during basic training in Texas. Shunned by fellow soldiers and permanently assigned to KP duty, Ben Kuroki later described the two of them as "the loneliest soldiers in the U.S. Army." Still, they refused to quit.

For nearly a year before the 100th Infantry Battalion arrived in Europe and began making headlines to echo the valor of the Japanese-American soldier in combat, Sergeant Ben Kuroki flew in the skies over Europe and North Africa. He flew more than the allotted 25 missions, 29 in all, most as a top turret gunner on a B-24 Liberator, including participating in the ill-fated bombing mission over the Ploesti oil fields. Wounded in his last mission, he returned home with an impressive array of medals including the

Distinguished Service Cross. He was featured in Time Magazine, hailed a hero by the War Department, and toured the internment camps as a popular speaker.

In 1944 Ben Kuroki requested assignment with the Army Air Force flying B-29 bombers over Japan. Despite his status as an American hero, he was initially denied. Only after enlisting support from one of his Nebraska senators did he finally get the assignment he sought. By war's end, Ben Kuroki had flown an incredible 58 bombing missions.

Because of the intense media praise heaped upon the soldiers of the 100th/442d Regimental Combat Team, one might quickly forget that Japanese-Americans fought elsewhere during World War II. While four of the five Masaoka brothers indeed fought with the Nisei Regiment, their fifth brother Henry fought with men of the 101st Airborne Division. (All five of the Masaoka brothers were wounded in action, and Ben Masaoka was killed in action during the rescue of the Lost Battalion. In all, the five brothers earned more than 30 combat decorations for their service.) And, scattered throughout other units, were other brave Nisei.

Some 6,000 Nisei served in the Pacific Theater of operations, but their exploits were less publicized and are still less known. Part of this stems from the fact that there was no single Japanese-American unit in the Pacific, the Nisei were scattered individually throughout other units. Another significant reason stems from the fact that most of those serving in the Pacific were working for MIS (Military Intelligence Service), in roles that were kept classified. The secrecy under which many of them served in the Pacific theater was so thorough, citations for the many awards earned by these patriots were brief, general, and in some cases non-existent. Even half a century after the end of World War II, the valor and exploits of these brave soldiers is still generally unknown to most Americans.

The fact remains that these brave soldiers fought in every battle and every campaign in the Pacific, in roles that became vital to victory.

The groundwork for the use of Nisei in the Pacific began in

earnest six months before Pearl Harbor. With diplomatic relations between the United States and Japan at a stalemate, the potential for hostilities between the two nations was obvious. The War Department began to secretly recruit Asian Americans living on the West Coast for use as Japanese-language interpreters and translators. When Pearl Harbor was attacked in December, nearly sixty of these soldiers were already undergoing specialized training in military intelligence and communications at the Presidio of San Francisco. Classes were held under the leadership of four Nisei instructors, and of the 60 initial students at the top-secret school, 58 were Japanese-Americans. By the spring of 1942 the first 35 graduates of the school were transferred to duty in the Pacific, serving in Guadalcanal and the Buna-Gona campaign.

While these were the first graduates of the MIS training program (and the largest initial group to be assigned to duty in the Pacific,) a similar program had also been underway in Hawaii. Young Nisei had been trained in the Corps of Intelligence Police (CIP) and Counter Intelligence Corps (CIC) early in 1941, and were already serving in the Pacific when the first 60 West Coast Nisei began their schooling. Richard Sakakida was serving as an interpreter in the Philippines by May of 1941, where he was also used by the CIP in clandestine espionage. When the Japanese attacked the Philippines shortly after Pearl Harbor, Sakakida was transferred to Bataan to translate Japanese documents obtained from captured or killed enemy soldiers. He served throughout the first dark months of the battle at Bataan, moving to Corregidor at the same time General MacArthur moved his headquarters to the island fortress. On May 6, 1942 it was Richard Sakakida who broadcast the surrender announcement in Japanese, and it was also Mr. Sakakida who accompanied General Jonathan Wainwright's Chief of Staff to meet the enemy in the surrender negotiation. After the fall of Corregidor, Sakakida suffered cruel torture at the hands of the Japanese, who found little sympathy for a man of Japanese ancestry serving in the uniform of the United States of America.

In the summer of 1942 the MIS linguistics school was moved to

Camp Savage, Minnesota where, by war's end close to 3,000 Nisei were trained for duty as interpreters in the Pacific. More than 2,000 of them actually served in the combat zones.

These Nisei interpreters faced unique challenges, not the least of which was the fact that, if separated from their white fellow-soldiers, they could be quickly mistaken for an enemy soldier who had disguised himself as an American soldier. For this reason, the Nisei interpreters often had bodyguards, and were carefully protected, as their service was highly valued.

General Douglas MacArthur maintained a small group of MIS graduates on his staff. In 1944 Japanese Admiral Yamamoto's successor, Admiral Fukudome was carrying battle plans for the

Brigadier Frank D. Merrill with two of his Nisei interpreters, Technical Sergeant Herbert Miyasaki and Technical Sergeant Akiji Yoshimura.

Japanese fleet when his airplane crashed in the Philippines. Translated by two Hawaiian-born Nisei, Technical Sergeant Yoshikazu Yamada and Staff Sergeant George Yamashiro, these documents became invaluable in planning for the Battle of the Philippine Sea, where Japanese air and sea power were literally crushed.

In the India-Burma Campaign, Nisei also served. General Frank Merrill of the 5307th Composite Unit (Merrill's Marauders) had fourteen Nisei working with him behind enemy lines throughout his heroic campaign. These were graduates of the MIS school, again serving in secretive roles unknown in most circles. In fact, when the movie Merrill's Marauders was filmed in 1962, these brave Japanese-Americans were erroneously identified in the movie as Filipino interpreters. All were Japanese-Americans.

Sergeant Roy Matsumoto was with General Merrill during the 15-day siege at Maggot Hill in the spring of 1944. One night, with only the darkness to shelter him, he crawled close enough to the enemy camp to hug the ground and eavesdrop on the enemy's plans for an attack the following morning. Such information became invaluable to General Merrill.

MORE THAN HALF a century after the end of World War II, with volumes of books, documentaries, and historical articles about American service during the war, two erroneous myths often remain concerning the service of the Japanese-Americans in the Pacific. The first is that the role of MIS linguistics was a relative safe position. Indeed, Sadao Munemori who was the only Japanese-American to receive the Medal of Honor during World War II, had declined MIS duty in order to be sent to a combat unit. This mis-conception of the role of the MIS graduates is quickly dispelled by the fact that three received Distinguished Service Crosses, many more won Silver Stars, and Purple Heart awards were spread liberally among the MIS graduates... many of them posthumous awards.

The second erroneous myth is that the role of linguistics was the only role the Nisei were allowed in the Pacific theater. Early in the war Lieutenant Colonel Harrison A. Gerhardt outlined three reasons the War Department was reluctant to commit Japanese-American soldiers to combat in the Pacific.

First, the enemy might put on the uniforms of dead American soldiers to infiltrate the ranks as American Nisei soldiers, thus wreaking havoc; Second, in the event a Japanese-American soldier was captured by the enemy, a substantial rick of severe torture was likely; and third, integrating Japanese-American soldiers into American units deployed to the Pacific would require extensive screening of each unit. (A not-so subtle indication of the suspicion that remained about the Japanese-Americans among ranking military leaders.)

Despite this official policy, nearly 4,000 Japanese-American soldiers (excluding the nearly 3,000 MIS graduates) served in combat theaters throughout the Pacific, landing with each new invasion, fighting honorably in each campaign, and leaving their blood on the beaches of islands like Guadalcanal, Saipan, Iwo Jima, and Okinawa.

Serving as interpreters for Japanese prisoners, Cpl. T. Torakawa and SSgt E. Kawamoto of the 3rd Marine Division at the battle for Iwo Jima,

Hoichi "Bob" Kubo gripped the rope tightly as he began to slide over the edge of the 100-foot cliff on the Island of Saipan. The Hawaiian-born Nisei soldier had faced danger before, had participated in the invasions of the Makin, Majuro, Saipan, and Tsugenjima. A few days earlier on July 7, 1944 the enemy had attacked in a banzai charge. Two American battalions of the 27th Infantry, short on ammunition, had been forced to pull back. The enemy pressed forward, assaulting the headquarters where Kubo worked as an interrogator and interpreter. American soldiers jumped into an anti-tank ditch and fired their weapons as the bodies of the suicidal enemy piled up around them. For days afterward Kubo's job called for him to sift through the bodies of the enemy for documents and papers that, when translated, might offer information helpful to American war planners.

As the Japanese fell back from the Islands that they had held, Kubo had one of the most dangerous jobs in the Pacific as a "cave flusher." The Pacific Islands were covered with deep caverns carved out of the lava that had created many of the islands. Into these caves fled the enemy, as well as the innocent Japanese civilians who populated the regions. Enemy propaganda had filled the civilians with great fear of the now advancing Americans, stories of mass torture, rape and mutilation of civilians at other islands that had fallen. So terrified were many of the civilians on these Pacific Islands that, as the Americans advanced, thousands committed suicide rather than endure the fate the Japanese soldiers warned would befall them at the hands of U.S. soldiers. In droves, young mothers clutching infants often plunged off high cliffs and into the sea to avoid becoming victims of the Americans. The senseless deaths of these civilians shocked the American soldiers. They were horrified at the sight of piles of bodies below the cliffs, and at the effectiveness of the enemy propaganda machine. Soldiers like Bob Kubo worked to discredit that propaganda machine and save civilian lives.

The Nisei cave flushers were effective in turning the tide of this propaganda, not only because they could speak the language of the civilians who retreated for safety to the deep caverns, but simply by their presence. Japanese soldiers had been told and believed, that the United States had executed all Japanese immigrants at the outbreak of World War II, in retaliation for Pearl Harbor. The appearance of a Japanese face in an American uniform was the first step in discrediting such reports both among the fleeing Japanese soldiers and the local civilian populace. Cave flushers repeatedly entered the caverns to speak to civilians in their native tongue, coaxing them to safety with assurances that the tales of the American atrocities were untrue.

As Bob Kubo slipped down the rope into yet another cave, he knew danger lurked ahead. Such caves usually held not only civilians, but frequently also contained enemy soldiers. On this day the group of 122 local women and children seeking refuge in the cavern also included eight enemy soldiers who were trapped with them. Armed only with a pistol, carefully hidden under his uniform, and carrying a case of C-rations, Bob Kubo slipped into the darkness to negotiate

Nisei interpreters use "hogen" (a local dialect) to successfully lure natives from caves in Okinawa, convincing them they are safe. MIS trained Nisei soldiers are credited for saving thousands of lives.

the surrender of the enemy and rescue the lives of the civilians. Alone, his greatest weapon would be his ability to think fast and speak their language.

Quickly Kubo built a rapport with the enemy soldiers, explaining that what they had heard about American treatment of prisoners was false. He shared his C-rations with the hungry, trapped Japanese. He gained their respect by relating to the enemy commander that his grandfathers had fought in the Sino-Japanese war. As the enemy came to grips with the unexpected appearance of a Japanese face in the uniform of a United States soldier, they asked how Kubo could fight for the Americans. Kubo's parents back in Hawaii had taken great pains to insure that their son, though American, would never lose a sense of his heritage. In that cave his understanding of Japanese history and culture served him well. He replied with a quote from ancestral lore when a son faced his father on a battlefield. When asked by the father how he could fight against him, the son replied: "If I am filial, I cannot serve the Emperor. If I serve the Emperor, I cannot be filial." It was a statement the enemy soldiers quickly recognized and understood. After four and a half hours, Bob Kubo emerged from the cave with eight prisoners, and 122 freed civilians.

It was actions such as these that vividly portray the heroism of the Nisei who served in the MIS. Bob Kubo had initially resisted assignment as a linguist, preferring to fight with his Nisei brothers in the 100th Infantry. "I tried to fail it," he later said of his exam for MIS training. "I didn't want to go to the Pacific and sit in a corner somewhere with a dictionary in my hand." Such was the impression of the role of the MIS graduates then, a myth many still believe today.

For his action in the cave at Saipan, Bob Kubo was awarded the Distinguished Service Cross. He went on to join his unit in the deadly assault at Okinawa, continuing his work of saving civilian lives. He was one of ten such Nisei "interpreters" serving in the 27th Division under the command of Second Lieutenant Benjamin Hazard. Hundreds more served in similar roles throughout the

Pacific. Kubo emerged from World War II the most decorated Japanese-American in the Pacific Theater.

The role of the MIS linguists was indeed a unique and challenging one. The young Nisei, often the only Japanese face in an American unit, were at first suspected and avoided, but later prized and protected. They experienced moments of incredible accomplishment as in the translation of captured, vital enemy war plans or the rescue of innocent civilians. They also endured moments of macabre duty, sifting through enemy bodies that were often bloated and decaying, searching for vital documents that might provide valuable intelligence. "There are things you want to forget," Bob Kubo said in a 1994 interview with the *Las Vegas Review-Journal.* "You want to make them vague. But some things you cannot forget."

And there were some moments when friend and foe were unable to be separated by a war that could not escape their heritage. Technician Third Grade Takejiro Higa had volunteered for service in Hawaii in 1943, and two years later found himself working as a linguist on Okinawa, ironically, it was the island where he had grown as a child.

One day as he sat before enemy prisoners to interrogate them, he found himself facing two of his former classmates from the 7th and 8th grades. Wearing the uniform of a United States soldier, the frightened Japanese prisoners hadn't recognized him. "Don't you recognize your own classmate?" He asked in surprise. "They looked up at me in total disbelief and then started crying, both in happiness and relief," Higa later recounted. "That hit me very hard and I, too, could not help but shed some tears."

Not all of the Asian faces behind American uniforms in the Pacific were Japanese. Thousands of Filipinos, both native and American, served throughout the Pacific Islands and elsewhere. Rudolph Davila of the 442d Regimental Combat Team in Italy and France was an American born of Hispanic and Filipino heritage. In the Philippine Islands, other Filipinos fought bravely for their homeland. Among them were the famed Filipino scouts that made up much of General Douglas MacArthur's valiant army. These citizens of the Philippines had been trained by American military instructors; carried weapons supplied by the United States, and were commanded in the field by American Army officers. They were a brave group of men who met the enemy when the Japanese invaded the Philippines in December 1941. Those who escaped capture continued to wage guerrilla warfare on the enemy until their homeland was again liberated.

Among the Filipino scouts at the time of the Japanese invasion on the peninsula of Bataan was a 34-year-old mess sergeant named Jose Calugas. Sergeant Calugas directed the efforts to feed the scouts who went into the jungles to meet and repel the advancing Japanese. On January 16, 1942 Sergeant Calugas had finished serving breakfast and was leading a detail of KPs to get water to clean up when Japanese artillery began landing in and around the large guns of his Battery B, 88th Field Artillery. The enemy barrage was followed by low level bombing attacks, as some 900 enemy soldiers half a mile north of the position began moving forward to attack.

For hours into the afternoon the enemy artillery continued to pound the small compound, forcing the men to remain under cover in nearby caves. When Sergeant Calugas noted that one of his battery's big guns had been knocked out, and its crew killed, he raced through 1,000 yards of open ground, heedless of the enemy fire, to round up volunteers to man the gun. As he moved his small band of volunteers toward the now silent artillery piece, enemy fire continued to fall on the area. By the time he reached the overturned big gun, Calugas was alone. Enlisting assistance from a wounded member of the original gun crew, he righted the heavy artillery piece. Then, for four hours, the Army mess sergeant single-handedly operated the gun, his effective fire keeping the enemy at bay.

On February 24, 1942 the general order announcing the award of the Medal of Honor to Sergeant Jose Calugas was read before the entire battery. The "Voice of Freedom" radio broadcast the account of his actions and pro-claimed him a hero. Two months later Bataan

Jose Calugas

fell to the Japanese, Sergeant Calugas himself becoming a prisoner of war. He survived three years as a captive of the Japanese, including the infamous Bataan Death March. On April 30, 1945 the repatriated hero finally received his Medal of Honor from General George C. Marshall at Pampanga, Camp Olivas, in the Philippine Islands.

Although Asian Americans served valiantly throughout both theaters of action during World War II, few were allowed combat leadership roles. Few and far between were officers like Captain Kim of the Purple Heart Battalion. Most Nisei and other Asian Americans served under white officers. One of the exceptions was Hawaii's Captain Francis B. Wai.

Wai was born of mixed ancestry; his mother a native Hawaiian, his father was Chinese. After graduating from Punahou School in Honolulu, young enrolled at the University of California in Los Angeles. He enlisted in the Hawaii National guard and was called to active duty in 1940. In 1941 he received his commission through OCS (Officer's Candidate School).

By the fall of 1944, Francis Wai was an Army captain assigned to Headquarters, 24th Infantry. On October 20th he landed with his unit at Read Beach on Leyte, in the Philippine Islands. It was the first steps in General MacArthur's return to the Philippines.

The attack on Leyte began early on the morning of the 20th with heavy aerial and Naval bombardment. At 1000 hours, the ground forces of X Corps, composed of the 24th Infantry and 1st Cavalry Divisions, began their amphibious assault near Palo on the north coast of Leyte. Captain Wai's men waded ashore at Red Beach. As they broke through the surf and crossed the open expanse of the sandy beach, the enemy opened fire. Hidden in a palm grove bounded by submerged rice paddies, the enemy had both concealment and a broad field of fire. Four waves of advancing American soldiers walked into their withering fire, all of their officers falling and the men reeling back in

Francis Wai

fear and confusion. Ignoring the enemy fire, Captain Wai moved forward, issued clear and concise commands, bringing order to the chaos among the first four ranks. He then began moving forward to assault their positions into the rice paddies, fully exposing himself to the enemy fire. Watching the lone officer proceed into the hail of death alone and determined to succeed, the men were inspired to rise up and follow. As they followed, Captain Wai repeatedly exposed himself to draw enemy fire and allow the advancing Americans to locate the hidden enemy and destroy them. One by one the Americans began to take the well-fortified Japanese positions. While assaulting the last remaining Japanese pillbox in the area, Captain Wai was killed. The vivid picture of his courage at Red Beach remained in the minds of his soldiers, continued to motivate them forward after his death. Before the initial assault was completed in those critical first 24 hours, the 24th Infantry Division moved a mile inland to secure their objectives along Highway 1. Out of the chaos that could have spelled disaster, the courageous Chinese-American had inspired incredible victory.

Captain Francis Wai was buried at the Punchbowl in Honolulu, and posthumously awarded the Distinguished Service Cross. He was the only Chinese-American of World War II to receive his nation's second highest award for combat valor. On June 21, 2000 when President Clinton awarded Medals of Honor to twenty Japanese-Americans and one Hispanic-Filipino for their World War II heroism, Francis Wai of Honolulu became the only Chinese- American Medal of Honor recipient of World War II.

On September 2, 1945 a contingent of Japanese government and military leaders slowly boarded the USS Missouri from their launch in Tokyo Harbor. Waiting for them on board was General Douglas MacArthur. Above their heads flew the American flag, ironically and appropriately, the same identical flag that was flying over our nation's Capitol on December 7, 1941 when World War II began. As they stepped to the table to sign the historic documents ending World War II, a line of Allied military leaders watched the historic proceedings. Among them stood the Nisei, graduates of MIS, called to interpret and translate the proceedings to end the war, just as they had so valiantly served to interpret and translate millions of pages of documents that led immeasurably to the Allied victory. Unfortunately, because of the secrecy within which many of them worked, few Americans would ever know the vital role they played by their sacrifice.

Retiring The Colors: The Long Road Home

"Blood that has soaked into the sands of a beach is all one color. America stands unique in the world, the only country not founded on race, but on a way—an ideal."

General Joseph "Vinegar Joe" Stilwell upon presenting a posthumous award of the Distinguished Service Cross to Mary Masuda, sister of Staff Sergeant Kazuo Masuda.

THE LAST, VICTORIOUS campaign of the 100th/442nd was a beautiful example of the teamwork and *Esprit de Corps* that existed in the Nisei unit. Unfortunately, not all members of the team were present to participate. In Germany the Teams 522d Field Artillery Battalion was still "on loan" to other units. The closing days of the war would provide the unit with one of their most haunting engagements of the war.

Many of the young soldiers of the 522d Field Artillery Battalion had come to the 442nd after enlisting at relocation camps in the Western United States. Many Japanese Americans who then populated the camps, as indeed do many even today, disliked the term "relocation camp." The hastily constructed facilities were laid out in a militaristic fashion with spartan surroundings. Around the camp were barbed wire and gun towers. While the government exercised great caution in censorship of the photographs taken of the camps, occasionally an embarrassing photo surfaced. Every effort had been expended to screen out photos that showed the Japanese interred there in the presence of army guards. But the fact remained, and a few uncensored photos proved, that these American citizens were indeed under armed guard. For all practical intents and purposes, these *relocation camps* were actually America's version of concentration camps.

As the Allied advance moved swiftly into the heart of Germany, the soldiers of the 522d once again saw similar facilities, spartan camps laid out in military fashion and surrounded by barbed wire and gun towers. The Nisei were among the first to enter the gates of the Dachau concentration camp where some of the most grotesque and inhumane medical experiments of the war were performed on living human beings... most of whom were Jewish. The liberation of Dachau provided a picture most of the Nisei would never forget, one that haunted them throughout their lives.

Under orders not to share supplies as the war was still in progress, the Nisei could not ignore the pleas of the human skeletons that paraded thankfully before them. As the Nisei handed out food from their own packs, sympathetic officers looked the other way. Sometimes, the heart demanded that one ignore orders and do what is right. Sadly, too many German soldiers had never learned this lesson, and the horrors of Dachau provided ample proof to attest this fact.

For the 522d's Central Europe Campaign from March 22 to May 11, 1945, the 552d Field Artillery Battalion added yet another *Presidential Unit Citation* to the incredible record of the 442d Regimental Combat Team. Shortly after the liberation of Dachau, the unit returned to Italy to join the rest of their team.

Over the next fourteen months, the 442nd remained in Italy to direct much of the postwar effort. Many of their duties after the May 9, 1945 German surrender

This once restricted photograph is that of Kiyoto Nakai, veteran of the 442nd RCT who was blinded in battle, with his arm around his fiance Miyaho Hiratoni. His "seeing-eye" dog, Cubby, sits patiently for the Signal Corps photographer to snap the photo

*Enlisted men from the 100th Bn happily awaiting
30 day furloughs and subsequent discharges. This entire group saw
action in Africa, Italy and Southern France, many of them hold the
Purple Heart and Presidential Citations*

were the guarding of prisoners of war. Immediately after the war
ended, nearly 200 combat veterans of the 100th/442d (including
four officers), volunteered for the MIS (now called MISLS - Military
Intelligence Service Language School) in order to serve in the
Pacific. Before the summer came to an end however, the Japanese
surrendered. With the historic signing aboard the USS Missouri in
Tokyo Harbor on September 2, 1945, all World War II hostilities
had terminated.

Without battles to wage, the focus of the Nisei unit changed. During the training phases for both the 100th Infantry Battalion and the
442d RCT in the days before combat, the Nisei units had stood out
for their military professionalism, pride, and military bearing. Now,
in the months before the expected return home, the unit turned once
again to close-order drills, spit-shines, starch, and inspections. In
the early months of 1946, the emphasis increased to an even greater

pitch. Not only was the 442d Regimental Combat Team going home, they were to be the *only* returning military unit to date to be received by the President of the United States.

On July 16, 1946 the proud Nisei of the 100th Infantry Battalion/ 442d Regimental combat team marched proudly down Constitution Avenue in Washington, DC. It was a festive day, more than 10,000 citizens braving the rain to watch the return of the most decorated unit of World War II, perhaps the most decorated in American military history.

Color Guard of the 442nd RCT. (L to R) Jitsuo Yoshida, Hisaji B. Hamamoto, Melvin Tshchya and Bill T. Nakada

Dignitaries and military officials abounded. The War Department and other Federal agencies gave employees special time off to witness the return of the Nisei. The proud "Go For Broke" regiment marched up Constitution to the White House lawn where they met their Commander in Chief. As the proud young soldiers stood rigidly at attention, the President removed his hat and placed it over his heart as he passed in review. Then he presented the unit with its unprecedented seventh *Presidential Unit Citation*. As he looked out over the proud, young faces of the Japanese-American soldiers, he spoke proudly of their service.

"You fought for the free nations of the world. You fought not only the enemy, you fought prejudice—and you won. Keep up that fight... continue to win—make this great Republic stand for what the Constitution says it stands for: 'the welfare of all the people, all the time.'"

President Harry S Truman
July 15, 1945

If we, the living, the beneficiaries of their sacrifices are truly intent upon showing our gratitude, we must do more than gather together for speechmaking and perfunctory ceremonies. We must undertake to carry on the unfinished work which they so nobly advanced. The fight against prejudice is not confined to the battlefield alone. It is here and with us now. So long as a single member of our citizenry is denied the use of public facilities and denied the right to earn a decent living because, and solely because of the color of his skin, we who 'fought against prejudice and won' ought not sit idly by and tolerate the perpetuation of injustices."

Senator Spark M. Matsunaga
A Purple Heart Veteran of the Purple Heart Bn.

Following the heraldic reception in our nation's Capitol, veterans of the 100th/442d began returning home. In August the 442d Regimental Combat Team was demobilized and inactivated. The lineage and honors have been preserved by the 100th Battalion, 442d Infantry (U.S. Army Reserve).

Even as World War II was drawing to a close, a group of freshly trained young Nisei was enroute as replacements for the 100th/442nd. The troop transport carrying the eager young soldiers to Italy was five days from shore when word arrived that the war was over. Among the new arrivals was a young Nisei from Gallup, New Mexico... Private Hiroshi H. Miyamura.

Young "Hershey," as he was called, served with the 100th/442nd during their post-war year in Italy, then returned to the United States with his victorious unit, never having seen combat. But the torch of liberty, together with a proud heritage, had been passed to a new generation of Japanese-Americans. Seven years later Hershey returned to battle on foreign shores, this time in Korea. There he fought with the same courage and determination that marked his brothers of World War II. In Korea, Hiroshi H. Miyamura became the second Japanese-American to receive the Medal of Honor, and until the DSCs of the World War II Nisei were upgraded on June 21, 2000, he was the only living Japanese-American Medal of Honor recipient.

Medal of Honor Citations

FROM ITS INCEPTION during the Civil War and through the Spanish-American War (1898), the Honor Roll of Medal Of Honor recipients reflected a wide diversity of American soldiers, from low ranking privates to top generals. Ethnic and cultural diversity was also reflected, the award going to Native Americans, Buffalo Soldiers, Hispanic Americans, Jewish heroes, and foreign immigrants. Awards of the Medal of Honor during the Korean and Vietnam Wars reflected a similar cross-section of America. Of the more than 500 Medals of Honor awarded during World War I and II, however, the same could not be said. Though Hispanic and Native Americans had received the award during the two World Wars, not a single Black American, one Filipino, and only one Japanese-American soldier was awarded the Medal of Honor.

This initially prompted a review of World War I Distinguished Service Cross awards to Black American soldiers. On April 24, 1991 President George Bush presented the Medal of Honor to the sisters of Corporal Freddie Stowers, a young black soldier killed in action during World War I. His actions had been deemed of sufficient valor to merit our nation's highest award. A similar review of Black American soldiers awarded the DSC in World War II followed and, on January 13, 1997, President Clinton presented Medals of Honor to seven Black heroes of World War II. Six of the awards were posthumous presentations accepted by surviving family members. Of the seven, only Vernon Baker had survived both the war and the interval of years, to personally receive his medal.

Unlike America's Black veterans of the two World Wars, the Japanese-Americans could claim one Medal of Honor during the period, the award presented to Sadao Munemori. (Even Munemori had initially been awarded the DSC, but Utah Senator Albert Thomas had pushed for its upgrade to the Medal of Honor shortly after the end of World War II.) In view of the impressive record of the Nisei in World War II and particularly the incredible accomplishments of the 100th Infantry Battalion/442d Regimental Combat Team, it was generally believed that there should have been more.

In 1996 Hawaii Senator Daniel Akaka sponsored legislation ordering the re-evaluation of World War II awards to Japanese-Americans, and other Asian/Pacific Islanders who fought in both theaters. On June 21, 2000 President Clinton awarded 22 Medals of Honor as a result of this action.

Of the 22 awards upgraded, all had received the Distinguished Service Cross except medic James Okubo, who had received the Silver Star (his commanders believed it was the highest award for which he was eligible as a medic.) Okubo's upgrade was pushed through Congress in separate legislation, and approved in time for his Medal of Honor to be presented with the other 21.

Of the 22 awardees of the Medal of Honor, ten were killed in action (nine in Europe and one in the Pacific). Of the remaining, only seven had survived the half-century interim to personally receive the Medal of Honor. The posthumous presentations were made to surviving family members. One such award was the posthumous presentation to Robert Kuroda. All four young men in the Kuroda family served in World War II. Ronald Kuroda accepted the Medal of Honor on behalf of his brother. Ronald had himself, received the Distinguished Service Cross during World War II.

The seven who survived to personally accept their Medals Of Honor from President Clinton are: Rudolph Davila, Barney Hajiro, Shizuya Hayashi, Daniel Inouye, Yeiki Kobashigawa, Yukio Okutsu, George Sakato.

Following are the medal citations (listed alphabetically) of 23 awardees mentioned throughout this book. An asterisk (*) indicates the person died in the performance of his act of heroism.

Davila, Rudolph B.

Rank and organization: Staff
Sergeant, U.S. Army, Company H,
7th Infantry. *Place and date*: Artena,
Italy, 28 May, 1944. *Born:* 27 April
1916, El Paso, TX *Entered service at:*
Los Angeles, Calif.

Citation:

Staff Sergeant Rudolph B. Davila distinguished himself by
extraordinary heroism in action, on 28 May 1944, near Artena, Italy.
During the offensive which broke through the German mountain
strongholds surrounding the Anzio beachhead, Staff Sergeant Davila
risked death to provide heavy weapons support for a beleaguered rifle
company. Caught on an exposed hillside by heavy, grazing fire from a
well-entrenched German force, his machine gunners were reluctant to
risk putting their guns into action. Crawling fifty yards to the nearest
machine gun, Staff Sergeant Davila set it up alone and opened fire on
the enemy. In order to observe the effect of his fire, Sergeant Davila
fired from the kneeling position, ignoring the enemy fire that struck
the tripod and passed between his legs. Ordering a gunner to take
over, he crawled forward to a vantage point and directed the firefight
with hand and arm signals until both hostile machine guns were
silenced. Bringing his three remaining machine guns into action, he
drove the enemy to a reserve position two hundred yards to the rear.
When he received a painful wound in the leg, he dashed to a burned
tank and, despite the crash of bullets on the hull, engaged a second
enemy force from the tank's turret. Dismounting, he advanced 130
yards in short rushes, crawled 20 yards and charged into an enemy-
held house to eliminate the defending force of five with a hand
grenade and rifle fire. Climbing to the attic, he attic, he straddled a
large shell hole in the wall and opened fire on the enemy. Although
the walls of the house were crumbling, he continued to fire until he
had destroyed two more machine guns. His intrepid actions brought
desperately needed heavy weapons support to a hard-pressed rifle
company and silenced four machine gunners, which forced the
enemy to abandon their prepared positions. Staff Sergeant Davila's
extraordinary heroism and devotion to duty are in keeping with the
highest traditions of military service and reflect great credit on him,
his unit, and the United States Army.

Hajiro, Barney F.

Rank and organization: Private, U.S. Army, Company I, 442nd Regimental Combat Team. *Place and date:* Bruyères and Biffontain, France, 19, 22 & 29 October, 1944. Born: 16 September 1916, Punene, Maui, Hawaii. *Entered service at:* Honolulu, Hawaii.

Citation:

Private Barney F. Hajiro distinguished himself by extraordinary heroism in action on 19, 22, and 29 October 1944, in the vicinity of Bruyères and Biffontaine, eastern France. Private Hajiro, while acting as a sentry on top of an embankment on 19 October 1944, in the vicinity of Bruyères, France, rendered assistance to allied troops attacking a house 200 yards away by exposing himself to enemy fire and directing fire at an enemy strong point. He assisted the unit on his right by firing his automatic rifle and killing or wounding two enemy snipers. On 22 October 1944, he and one comrade took up an outpost security position about 50 yards to the right front of their platoon, concealed themselves, and ambushed an 18-man, heavily armed, enemy patrol, killing two, wounding one, and taking the remainder as prisoners. On 29 October 1944, in a wooded area in the vicinity of Biffontaine, France, Private Hajiro initiated an attack up the slope of a hill referred to as "Suicide Hill" by running forward approximately 100 yards under fire. He then advanced ahead of his comrades about 10 yards, drawing fire and spotting camouflaged machine gun nests. He fearlessly met fire with fire and single-handedly destroyed two machine gun nests and killed two enemy snipers. As a result of Private Hajiro's heroic actions, the attack was successful. Private Hajiro's extraordinary heroism and devotion to duty are in keeping with the highest traditions of military service and reflect great credit upon him, his unit, and the United States Army.

*Hasemoto, Mikio

Rank and organization: Private, U.S. Army, Company B, 100th Infantry Battalion (Separate). *Place and date*: Cerasuolo, Italy, 29 November 1943. *Born:* 13 July 1916, Honolulu, Hawaii. *Entered service at:* Schofield Barracks, Hawaii.

Citation:

Private Mikio Hasemoto distinguished himself by extraordinary heroism in action on 29 November 1943, in the vicinity of Cerasuolo, Italy. A force of approximately 40 enemy soldiers, armed with machine guns, machine pistols, rifles, and grenades, attacked the left flank of his platoon. Two enemy soldiers with machine guns advanced forward, firing their weapons. Private Hasemoto, an automatic rifleman, challenged these two machine gunners. After firing four magazines at the approaching enemy, his weapon was shot and damaged. Unhesitatingly, he ran ten yards to the rear, secured another automatic rifle and continued to fire until his weapon jammed. At this point, Private Hasemoto and his squad leader had killed approximately 20 enemy soldiers. Again, Private Hasemoto ran through a barrage of enemy machine gun fire to pick up an M-1 rifle. Continuing their fire, Private Hasemoto and his squad leader killed ten more enemy soldiers. With only three enemy soldiers left, he and his squad leader charged courageously forward, killing one, wounding one, and capturing another. The following day, Private Hasemoto continued to repel enemy attacks until he was killed by enemy fire. Private Hasemoto's extraordinary heroism and devotion to duty are in keeping with the highest traditions of military service and reflect great credit on him, his unit, and the United States Army.

*Hayashi, Joe

Rank and organization: Private, U.S. Army, Company K, 442nd Regimental Combat Team. *Place and date*: Tendola, Italy, 20 & 22 April 1945. *Born:* 14 August 1920, Salinas, Calif. *Entered service at:* Pasadena, Calif.

Citation:

Private Joe Hayashi distinguished himself by extraordinary heroism in action on 20 and 22 April 1945, near Tendola, Italy. On 20 April 1945, ordered to attack a strongly defended hill that commanded all approaches to the village of Tendola, Private Hayashi skillfully led his men to a point within 75 yards of enemy positions before they were detected and fired upon. After dragging his wounded comrades to safety, he returned alone and exposed himself to small arms fire in order to direct and adjust mortar fire against hostile emplacements. Boldly attacking the hill with the remaining men of his squad, he attained his objective and discovered that the mortars had neutralized three machine guns, killed 27 men, and wounded many others. On 22 April 1945, attacking the village of Tendola, Private Hayashi maneuvered his squad up a steep, terraced hill to within 100 yards of the enemy. Crawling under intense fire to a hostile machine gun position, he threw a grenade, killing one enemy soldier and forcing the other members of the gun crew to surrender. Seeing four enemy machine guns delivering deadly fire upon other elements of his platoon, he threw another grenade, destroying a machine gun nest. He then crawled to the right flank of another machine gun position where he killed four enemy soldiers and forced the others to flee. Attempting to pursue the enemy, he was mortally wounded by a burst of machine pistol fire. The dauntless courage and exemplary leadership of Private Hayashi enabled his company to attain its objective. Private Hayashi's extraordinary heroism and devotion to duty are in keeping with the highest traditions of military service and reflect great credit on him, his unit, and the United States Army.

Hayashi, Shizuya

Rank and organization: Private, U.S. Army, Company A, 100th Infantry Battalion (Separate). *Place and date*: Cerasuolo, Italy, 29 November 1943. *Born:* 28 November 1917, Waialua, Oahu, Hawaii *Entered service at:* Schofield Barracks, Hawaii.

Citation:

Private Shizuya Hayashi distinguished himself by extraordinary heroism in action on 29 November 1943, near Cerasuolo, Italy. During a flank assault on high ground held by the enemy, Private Hayashi rose alone in the face of grenade, rifle, and machine gun fire. Firing his automatic rifle from the hip, he charged and overtook an enemy machine gun position, killing seven men in the nest and two more as they fled. After his platoon advanced 200 yards from this point, an enemy antiaircraft gun opened fire on the men. Private Hayashi returned fire at the hostile position, killing nine of the enemy, taking four prisoners, and forcing the remainder of the force to withdraw from the hill. Private Hayashi's extraordinary heroism and devotion to duty are in keeping with the highest traditions of military service and reflect great credit on him, his unit, and the United States Army.

Inouye, Daniel K.

Rank and organization: Second Lieutenant, U.S. Army, Company E, 442nd Infantry. *Place and date*: San Terenzo, Italy, 21 April 1945. *Birth*: 7 September 1924, Honolulu, Hawaii. *Entered service at:* Honolulu, Hawaii.

Citation:

Second Lieutenant Daniel K. Inouye distinguished himself by extraordinary heroism in action on 21 April 1945, in the vicinity of San Terenzo, Italy. While attacking a defended ridge guarding an important road junction, Second Lieutenant Inouye skillfully directed his platoon through a hail of automatic weapon and small arms fire, in a swift enveloping movement that resulted in the capture of an artillery and mortar post and brought his men to within 40 yards of the hostile force. Emplaced in bunkers and rock formations, the enemy halted the advance with crossfire from three machine guns. With complete disregard for his personal safety, Second Lieutenant Inouye crawled up the treacherous slope to within five yards of the nearest machine gun and hurled two grenades, destroying the emplacement. Before the enemy could retaliate, he stood up and neutralized a second machine gun nest. Although wounded by a sniper's bullet, he continued to engage other hostile positions at close range until an exploding grenade shattered his right arm. Despite the intense pain, he refused evacuation and continued to direct his platoon until enemy resistance was broken and his men were again deployed in defensive positions. In the attack, 25 enemy soldiers were killed and eight others captured. By his gallant, aggressive tactics and by his indomitable leadership, Second Lieutenant Inouye enabled his platoon to advance through formidable resistance, and was instrumental in the capture of the ridge. Second Lieutenant Inouye's extraordinary heroism and devotion to duty are in keeping with the highest traditions of military service and reflect great credit on him, his unit, and the United States Army.

*Kuroda, Robert T.

Rank and organization: Staff Sergeant, U.S. Army, Company H, 442nd Regimental Combat Team. *Place and date*: Bruyères, France, 20 October 1944. *Birth*: 8 November 1922, Aiea, Oahu, Hawaii. *Entered service at:* Honolulu, Hawaii.

Citation:

Staff Sergeant Robert T. Kuroda distinguished himself by extraordinary heroism in action, on 20 October 1944, near Bruyères, France. Leading his men in an advance to destroy snipers and machine gun nests, Staff Sergeant Kuroda encountered heavy fire from enemy soldiers occupying a heavily wooded slope. Unable to pinpoint the hostile machine gun, he boldly made his way through heavy fire to the crest of the ridge. Once he located the machine gun, Staff Sergeant Kuroda advanced to a point within ten yards of the nest and killed three enemy gunners with grenades. He then fired clip after clip of rifle ammunition, killing or wounding at least three of the enemy. As he expended the last of his ammunition, he observed that an American officer had been struck by a burst of fire from a hostile machine gun located on an adjacent hill. Rushing to the officer's assistance, he found that the officer had been killed. Picking up the officer's submachine gun, Staff Sergeant Kuroda advanced through continuous fire toward a second machine gun emplacement and destroyed the position. As he turned to fire upon additional enemy soldiers, he was killed by a sniper. Staff Sergeant Kuroda's courageous actions and indomitable fighting spirit ensured the destruction of enemy resistance in the sector. Staff Sergeant Kuroda's extraordinary heroism and devotion to duty are in keeping with the highest traditions of military service and reflect great credit on him, his unit, and the United States Army.

Kobashigawa, Yeiki

Rank and organization: Technical Sergeant, U.S. Army, Company B, 100th Infantry Battalion (Separate). *Place and date:* Lanuvio, Italy, 2 June 1944. Birth: 28 September 1917, Hilo, Hawaii Entered service at: Honolulu, Hawaii.

Citation:

Technical Sergeant Yeiki Kobashigawa distinguished himself by extraordinary heroism in action on 2 June 1944, in the vicinity of Lanuvio, Italy. During an attack, Technical Sergeant Kobashigawa's platoon encountered strong enemy resistance from a series of machine guns providing supporting fire. Observing a machine gun nest 50 yards from his position, Technical Sergeant Kobashigawa crawled forward with one of his men, threw a grenade and then charged the enemy with his submachine gun while a fellow soldier provided covering fire. He killed one enemy soldier and captured two prisoners. Meanwhile, Technical Sergeant Kobashigawa and his comrade were fired upon by another machine gun 50 yards ahead. Directing a squad to advance to his first position, Technical Sergeant Kobashigawa again moved forward with a fellow soldier to subdue the second machine gun nest. After throwing grenades into the position, Technical Sergeant Kobashigawa provided close supporting fire while a fellow soldier charged, capturing four prisoners. On the alert for other machine gun nests, Technical Sergeant Kobashigawa discovered four more, and skillfully led a squad in neutralizing two of them. Technical Sergeant Kobashigawa's extraordinary heroism and devotion to duty are in keeping with the highest traditions of military service and reflect great credit on him, his unit, and the United States Army.

*Munemori, Sadao S.

Rank and organization: Private First Class, U.S. Army, Company A,100th Infantry Battalion, 442d Combat Team. *Place and date*: Near Seravezza, Italy, 5 April 1945. *Entered service at*: Los Angeles, Calif. *Birth*: Los Angeles, Calif. *G.O. No.*. 24, 7 March 1946.

Citation:

He fought with great gallantry and intrepidity near Seravezza, Italy. When his unit was pinned down by grazing fire from the enemy's strong mountain defense and command of the squad devolved on him with the wounding of its regular leader, he made frontal, l-man attacks through direct fire and knocked out two machine guns with grenades Withdrawing under murderous fire and showers of grenades from other enemy emplacements, he had nearly reached a shell crater occupied by two of his men when an unexploded grenade bounced on his helmet and rolled toward his helpless comrades. He arose into the withering fire, dived for the missile and smothered its blast with his body. By his swift, supremely heroic action PFC Munemori saved two of his men at the cost of his own life and did much to clear the path for his company's victorious advance

*Moto, Kaoru

Rank and organization: Private First Class, U.S. Army, Company C, 100th Infantry Battalion (Separate). *Place and date*: Castellina, Italy, 7 July, 1944. *Birth*: Hawaii. *Entered service at:* Spreckelsville, Maui, Hawaii.

Citation:

Private First Class Kaoru Moto distinguished himself by extraordinary heroism in action on 7 July 1944, near Castellina, Italy. While serving as first scout, Private First Class Moto observed a machine gun nest that was hindering his platoon's progress. On his own initiative, he made his way to a point ten paces from the hostile position, and killed the enemy machine gunner. Immediately, the enemy assistant gunner opened fire in the direction of Private First Class Moto. Crawling to the rear of the position, Private First Class Moto surprised the enemy soldier, who quickly surrendered. Taking his prisoner with him, Private First Class Moto took a position a few yards from a house to prevent the enemy from using the building as an observation post. While guarding the house and his prisoner, he observed an enemy machine gun team moving into position. He engaged them, and with deadly fire forced the enemy to withdraw. An enemy sniper located in another house fired at Private First Class Moto, severely wounding him. Applying first aid to his wound, he changed position to elude the sniper fire and to advance. Finally relieved of his position, he made his way to the rear for treatment. Crossing a road, he spotted an enemy machine gun nest. Opening fire, he wounded two of the three soldiers occupying the position. Not satisfied with this accomplishment, he then crawled forward to a better position and ordered the enemy soldier to surrender. Receiving no answer, Private First Class Moto fired at the position, and the soldiers surrendered. Private First Class Moto's extraordinary heroism and devotion to duty are in keeping with the highest traditions of military service and reflect great credit on him, his unit, and the United States Army.

*Muranaga, Kiyoshi K.

Rank and organization: Private First Class, U.S. Army, Company F, 442nd Infantry. *Place and date*: Suvereto, Italy, 26 June 1944. *Born*: Lost Angeles, Calif. *Entered service at*: Ameche, Colo.

Citation:

Private First Class Kiyoshi K. Muranaga distinguished himself by extraordinary heroism in action on 26 June 1944, near Suvereto, Italy. Private First Class Muranaga's company encountered a strong enemy force in commanding positions and with superior firepower. An enemy 88mm self-propelled gun opened direct fire on the company, causing the men to disperse and seek cover. Private First Class Muranaga's mortar squad was ordered to action, but the terrain made it impossible to set up their weapons. The squad leader, realizing the vulnerability of the mortar position, moved his men away from the gun to positions of relative safety. Because of the heavy casualties being inflicted on his company, Private First Class Muranaga, who served as a gunner, attempted to neutralize the 88mm weapon alone. Voluntarily remaining at his gun position, Private First Class Muranaga manned the mortar himself and opened fire on the enemy gun at a range of approximately 400 yards. With his third round, he was able to correct his fire so that the shell landed directly in front of the enemy gun. Meanwhile, the enemy crew, immediately aware of the source of mortar fire, turned their 88mm weapon directly on Private First Class Muranaga's position. Before Private First Class Muranaga could fire a fourth round, an 88mm shell scored a direct hit on his position, killing him instantly. Because of the accuracy of Private First Class Muranaga's previous fire, the enemy soldiers decided not to risk further exposure and immediately abandoned their position. Private First Class Muranaga's extraordinary heroism and devotion to duty are in keeping with the highest traditions of military service and reflect great credit on him, his unit, and the United States Army.

*Nakae, Masato

Rank and organization: Private, U.S. Army, Company A, 100th/442nd Infantry. *Place and date*: Pisa, Italy, 19 August 1944. *Birth*: Lihue, Kauai, Hawaii. *Entered service at:* Honolulu, Hawaii.

Citation:

Private Masato Nakae distinguished himself by extraordinary heroism in action on 19 August 1944, near Pisa, Italy. When his submachine gun was damaged by a shell fragment during a fierce attack by a superior enemy force, Private Nakae quickly picked up his wounded comrade's M-1 rifle and fired rifle grenades at the steadily advancing enemy. As the hostile force continued to close in on his position, Private Nakae threw six grenades and forced them to withdraw. During a concentrated enemy mortar barrage that preceded the next assault by the enemy force, a mortar shell fragment seriously wounded Private Nakae. Despite his injury, he refused to surrender his position and continued firing at the advancing enemy. By inflicting heavy casualties on the enemy force, he finally succeeded in breaking up the attack and caused the enemy to withdraw. Private Nakae's extraordinary heroism and devotion to duty are in keeping with the highest traditions of military service and reflect great credit on him, his unit, and the United States Army.

*Nakamine, Shinyei

Rank and organization: Private, U.S. Army, Company B, 100th Infantry Battalion (Separate). *Place and date*: La Torreto, Italy, 2 June 1944. *Birth*: 21 January 1920, Waianae, Oahu, Hawaii. *Entered service at:* Honolulu, Hawaii.

Citation:

Private Shinyei Nakamine distinguished himself by extraordinary heroism in action on 2 June 1944, near La Torreto, Italy. During an attack, Private Nakamine's platoon became pinned down by intense machine gun crossfire from a small knoll 200 yards to the front. On his own initiative, Private Nakamine crawled toward one of the hostile weapons. Reaching a point 25 yards from the enemy, he charged the machine gun nest, firing his submachine gun, and killed three enemy soldiers and captured two. Later that afternoon, Private Nakamine discovered an enemy soldier on the right flank of his platoon's position. Crawling 25 yards from his position, Private Nakamine opened fire and killed the soldier. Then, seeing a machine gun nest to his front approximately 75 yards away, he returned to his platoon and led an automatic rifle team toward the enemy. Under covering fire from his team, Private Nakamine crawled to a point 25 yards from the nest and threw hand grenades at the enemy soldiers, wounding one and capturing four. Spotting another machine gun nest 100 yards to his right flank, he led the automatic rifle team toward the hostile position but was killed by a burst of machine gun fire. Private Nakamine's extraordinary heroism and devotion to duty are in keeping with the highest traditions of military service and reflect great credit on him, his unit, and the United States Army.

*Nakamura, William K.

Rank and organization: Private First Class, U.S. Army, Company G, 442nd Infantry. *Place and date*: Castellina, Italy. Born: 21 January 1922, Seattle, Wash. *Entered service at*: Minidoka Relocation Center, Hunt, Idaho

Citation:

Private First Class William K. Nakamura distinguished himself by extraordinary heroism in action on 4 July 1944, near Castellina, Italy. During a fierce firefight, Private First Class Nakamura's platoon became pinned down by enemy machine gun fire from a concealed position. On his own initiative, Private First Class Nakamura crawled 20 yards toward the hostile nest with fire from the enemy machine gun barely missing him. Reaching a point 15 yards from the position, he quickly raised himself to a kneeling position and threw four hand grenades, killing or wounding at least three of the enemy soldiers. The enemy weapon silenced, Private First Class Nakamura crawled back to his platoon, which was able to continue its advance as a result of his courageous action. Later, his company was ordered to withdraw from the crest of a hill so that a mortar barrage could be placed on the ridge. On his own initiative, Private First Class Nakamura remained in position to cover his comrades' withdrawal. While moving toward the safety of a wooded draw, his platoon became pinned down by deadly machine gun fire. Crawling to a point from which he could fire on the enemy position, Private First Class Nakamura quickly and accurately fired his weapon to pin down the enemy machine gunners. His platoon was then able to withdraw to safety without further casualties. Private First Class Nakamura was killed during this heroic stand. Private First Class Nakamura's extraordinary heroism and devotion to duty are in keeping with the highest traditions of military service and reflect great credit on him, his unit, and the United States Army.

*Nishimoto, Joe M.

Rank and organization: Private First Class, U.S. Army, Company G, 442nd Regimental Combat Team. *Place and date*: La Houssiere, France, 7 November 1944. *Born:* Fresno, Calif. *Entered service at:* Marion, Ohio.

Citation:

Private First Class Joe M. Nishimoto distinguished himself by extraordinary heroism in action on 7 November 1944, near La Houssiere, France. After three days of unsuccessful attempts by his company to dislodge the enemy from a strongly defended ridge, Private First Class Nishimoto, as acting squad leader, boldly crawled forward through a heavily mined and booby-trapped area. Spotting a machine gun nest, he hurled a grenade and destroyed the emplacement. Then, circling to the rear of another machine gun position, he fired his submachine gun at point-blank range, killing one gunner and wounding another. Pursuing two enemy riflemen, Private First Class Nishimoto killed one, while the other hastily retreated. Continuing his determined assault, he drove another machine gun crew from its position. The enemy, with their key strong points taken, were forced to withdraw from this sector. Private First Class Nishimoto's extraordinary heroism and devotion to duty are in keeping with the highest traditions of military service and reflect great credit on him, his unit, and the United States Army.

*Ohata, Allan M.

Rank and organization: Staff Sergeant, U.S. Army, Company B, 100th Infantry Battalion (Separate). *Place and date*: Cerasuolo, Italy, 29-30 November, 1943. *Born*: 13 September 1918, Honolulu, Hawaii. *Entered service at:* Honolulu, Hawaii.

Citation:

Sergeant Allan M. Ohata distinguished himself by extraordinary heroism in action on 29 and 30 November 1943, near Cerasuolo, Italy. Sergeant Ohata, his squad leader, and three men were ordered to protect his platoon's left flank against an attacking enemy force of 40 men, armed with machine guns, machine pistols, and rifles. He posted one of his men, an automatic rifleman, on the extreme left, 15 yards from his own position. Taking his position, Sergeant Ohata delivered effective fire against the advancing enemy. The man to his left called for assistance when his automatic rifle was shot and damaged. With utter disregard for his personal safety, Sergeant Ohata left his position and advanced 15 yards through heavy machine gun fire. Reaching his comrade's position, he immediately fired upon the enemy, killing ten enemy soldiers and successfully covering his comrade's withdrawal to replace his damaged weapon. Sergeant Ohata and the automatic rifleman held their position and killed 37 enemy soldiers. Both men then charged the three remaining soldiers and captured them. Later, Sergeant Ohata and the automatic rifleman stopped another attacking force of 14, killing four and wounding three while the others fled. The following day he and the automatic rifleman held their flank with grim determination and staved off all attacks. Staff Sergeant Ohata's extraordinary heroism and devotion to duty are in keeping with the highest traditions of military service and reflect great credit on him, his unit, and the United States Army.

*Ono, Frank H.

Rank and organization: Private First Class, U.S. Army, Company G, 442nd Regimental Combat Team. *Place and date*: Castellina, Italy, 4 July 1944. *Entered service at:* North Judson, Indiana

Citation:

Private First Class Frank H. Ono distinguished himself by extraordinary heroism in action on 4 July 1944, near Castellina, Italy. In attacking a heavily defended hill, Private First Class Ono's squad was caught in a hail of formidable fire from the well-entrenched enemy. Private First Class Ono opened fire with his automatic rifle and silenced one machine gun 300 hundred yards to the right front. Advancing through incessant fire, he killed a sniper with another burst of fire, and while his squad leader reorganized the rest of the platoon in the rear, he alone defended the critical position. His weapon was then wrenched from his grasp by a burst of enemy machine pistol fire as enemy troops attempted to close in on him. Hurling hand grenades, Private First Class Ono forced the enemy to abandon the attempt, resolutely defending the newly won ground until the rest of the platoon moved forward. Taking a wounded comrade's rifle, Private First Class Ono again joined in the assault. After killing two more enemy soldiers, he boldly ran through withering automatic, small arms, and mortar fire to render first aid to his platoon leader and a seriously wounded rifleman. In danger of being encircled, the platoon was ordered to withdraw. Volunteering to cover the platoon, Private First Class Ono occupied virtually unprotected positions near the crest of the hill, engaging an enemy machine gun emplaced on an adjoining ridge and exchanging fire with snipers armed with machine pistols. Completely disregarding his own safety, he made himself the constant target of concentrated enemy fire until the platoon reached the comparative safety of a draw. He then descended the hill in stages, firing his rifle, until he rejoined the platoon. Private First Class Ono's extraordinary heroism and devotion to duty are in keeping with the highest traditions of military service and reflect great credit on him, his unit, and the United States Army.

Okutsu, Yukio

Rank and organization: Technical Sergeant, U.S. Army, Company F, 442nd Regimental Combat Team. *Place and date*: Mount Belvedere, Italy, 7 April 1945. *Born*: 3 November 1921, Koloa, Kauai, Hawaii. *Entered service at:* Koloa, Kauai, Hawaii.

Citation:

Technical Sergeant Yukio Okutsu distinguished himself by extraordinary heroism in action on 7 April 1945, on Mount Belvedere, Italy. While his platoon was halted by the crossfire of three machine guns, Technical Sergeant Okutsu boldly crawled to within 30 yards of the nearest enemy emplacement through heavy fire. He destroyed the position with two accurately placed hand grenades, killing three machine gunners. Crawling and dashing from cover to cover, he threw another grenade, silencing a second machine gun, wounding two enemy soldiers, and forcing two others to surrender. Seeing a third machine gun, which obstructed his platoon's advance, he moved forward through heavy small arms fire and was stunned momentarily by rifle fire, which glanced off his helmet. Recovering, he bravely charged several enemy riflemen with his submachine gun, forcing them to withdraw from their positions. Then, rushing the machine gun nest, he captured the weapon and its entire crew of four. By these single-handed actions he enabled his platoon to resume its assault on a vital objective. The courageous performance of Technical Sergeant Okutsu against formidable odds was an inspiration to all. Technical Sergeant Okutsu's extraordinary heroism and devotion to duty are in keeping with the highest traditions of military service and reflect great credit on him, his unit, and the United States Army.

*Okubo, James K

Rank and organization: Technician Fifth Grade, U.S. Army, 442nd Regimental Combat Team. *Place and date*: near Biffontaine, France, 28-29 October and 4 November, 1944. *Entered service at:* Bellingham, Wash.

Citation:

Technician Fifth Grade James K. Okubo distinguished himself by extraordinary heroism in action on 28 and 29 October and 4 November 1944, in the Foret Domaniale de Champ, near Biffontaine, eastern France. On 28 October, under strong enemy fire coming from behind mine fields and roadblocks, Technician Fifth Grade Okubo, a medic, crawled 150 yards to within 40 yards of the enemy lines. Two grenades were thrown at him while he left his last covered position to carry back wounded comrades. Under constant barrages of enemy small arms and machine gun fire, he treated 17 men on 28 October and eight more men on 29 October. On 4 November, Technician Fifth Grade Okubo ran 75 yards under grazing machine gun fire and, while exposed to hostile fire directed at him, evacuated and treated a seriously wounded crewman from a burning tank, who otherwise would have died. Technician Fifth Grade James K. Okubo's extraordinary heroism and devotion to duty are in keeping with the highest traditions of military service and reflect great credit on him, his unit, and the United States Army.

*Otani, Kazuo

Rank and organization: Staff Sergeant, U.S. Army, Company G, 442nd Infantry. *Place and date*: Pieve di S. Luce, Italy, 15 July 1944. *Born*: Visalia, Calif. *Entered service at*: Rivers Relocation Center, Ariz.

Citation:

Staff Sergeant Kazuo Otani distinguished himself by extraordinary heroism in action on 15 July 1944, near Pieve Di S. Luce, Italy. Advancing to attack a hill objective, Staff Sergeant Otani's platoon became pinned down in a wheat field by concentrated fire from enemy machine gun and sniper positions. Realizing the danger confronting his platoon, Staff Sergeant Otani left his cover and shot and killed a sniper who was firing with deadly effect upon the platoon. Followed by a steady stream of machine gun bullets, Staff Sergeant Otani then dashed across the open wheat field toward the foot of a cliff, and directed his men to crawl to the cover of the cliff. When the movement of the platoon drew heavy enemy fire, he dashed along the cliff toward the left flank, exposing himself to enemy fire. By attracting the attention of the enemy, he enabled the men closest to the cliff to reach cover. Organizing these men to guard against possible enemy counterattack, Staff Sergeant Otani again made his way across the open field, shouting instructions to the stranded men while continuing to draw enemy fire. Reaching the rear of the platoon position, he took partial cover in a shallow ditch and directed covering fire for the men who had begun to move forward. At this point, one of his men became seriously wounded. Ordering his men to remain under cover, Staff Sergeant Otani crawled to the wounded soldier who was lying on open ground in full view of the enemy. Dragging the wounded soldier to a shallow ditch, Staff Sergeant Otani proceeded to render first aid treatment, but was mortally wounded by machine gun fire. Staff Sergeant Otani's extraordinary heroism and devotion to duty are in keeping with the highest traditions of military service and reflect great credit on him, his unit, and the United States Army.

Sakato, George T.

Rank and organization: Private, U.S. Army, Company E, 442nd Regimental Combat Team. *Place and date*: Biffontaine, France, 29 October, 1944. *Born:* 19 February 1921, Colcon, CA *Entered service at:* Glendale, Ariz.

Citation:

Private George T. Sakato distinguished himself by extraordinary heroism in action on 29 October 1944, on hill 617 in the vicinity of Biffontaine, France. After his platoon had virtually destroyed two enemy defense lines, during which he personally killed five enemy soldiers and captured four, his unit was pinned down by heavy enemy fire. Disregarding the enemy fire, Private Sakato made a one-man rush that encouraged his platoon to charge and destroy the enemy strongpoint. While his platoon was reorganizing, he proved to be the inspiration of his squad in halting a counter-attack on the left flank during which his squad leader was killed. Taking charge of the squad, he continued his relentless tactics, using an enemy rifle and P-38 pistol to stop an organized enemy attack. During this entire action, he killed twelve and wounded two, personally captured four and assisted his platoon in taking 34 prisoners. By continuously ignoring enemy fire, and by his gallant courage and fighting spirit, he turned impending defeat into victory and helped his platoon complete its mission. Private Sakato's extraordinary heroism and devotion to duty are in keeping with the highest traditions of military service and reflect great credit on him, his unit, and the United States Army.

*Tanouye, Ted T.

Rank and organization: Technical Sergeant, U.S. Army, Company K, 442nd Infantry. *Place and date:* Molina A Ventoabbto, Italy 7 July 1944. *Born:* Torrance, Calif. *Entered service at:* Fort MacArthur, Calif.

Citation:

Technical Sergeant Ted T. Tanouye distinguished himself by extraordinary heroism in action on 7 July 1944, near Molino A Ventoabbto, Italy. Technical Sergeant Tanouye led his platoon in an attack to capture the crest of a strategically important hill that afforded little cover. Observing an enemy machine gun crew placing its gun in position to his left front, Technical Sergeant Tanouye crept forward a few yards and opened fire on the position, killing or wounding three and causing two others to disperse. Immediately, an enemy machine pistol opened fire on him. He returned the fire and killed or wounded three more enemy soldiers. While advancing forward, Technical Sergeant Tanouye was subjected to grenade bursts, which severely wounded his left arm. Sighting an enemy-held trench, he raked the position with fire from his submachine gun and wounded several of the enemy. Running out of ammunition, he crawled 20 yards to obtain several clips from a comrade on his left flank. Next, sighting an enemy machine pistol that had pinned down his men, Technical Sergeant Tanouye crawled forward a few yards and threw a hand grenade into the position, silencing the pistol. He then located another enemy machine gun firing down the slope of the hill, opened fire on it, and silenced that position. Drawing fire from a machine pistol nest located above him, he opened fire on it and wounded three of its occupants. Finally taking his objective, Technical Sergeant Tanouye organized a defensive position on the reverse slope of the hill before accepting first aid treatment and evacuation. Technical Sergeant Tanouye's extraordinary heroism and devotion to duty are in keeping with the highest traditions of military service and reflect great credit on him, his unit, and the United States Army.

Wai, Francis

*Rank and organization:*Captain, U.S. Army, Headquarters, 34th Infantry, *Place and date*: Leyte, Philippine Islands, 20 October 1944
Entered service at: Honolulu, Hawaii
Born: Honolulu, Hawaii

Citation:

Captain Francis B. Wai distinguished himself by extraordinary heroism in action, on 20 October 1944, in Leyte, Philippine Islands. Captain Wai landed at Red Beach, Leyte, in the face of accurate, concentrated enemy fire from gun positions advantageously located in a palm grove bounded by submerged rice paddies. Finding the first four waves of American soldiers leaderless, disorganized, and pinned down on the open beach, he immediately assumed command. Issuing clear and concise orders, and disregarding heavy enemy machine gun and rifle fire, he began to move inland through the rice paddies without cover. The men, inspired by his cool demeanor and heroic example, rose from their positions and followed him. During the advance, Captain Wai repeatedly determined the locations of enemy strong points by deliberately exposing himself to draw their fire. In leading an assault upon the last remaining Japanese pillbox in the area, he was killed by its occupants. Captain Wai's courageous, aggressive leadership inspired the men, even after his death, to advance and destroy the enemy. His intrepid and determined efforts were largely responsible for the rapidity with which the initial beachhead was secured. Captain Wai's extraordinary heroism and devotion to duty are in keeping with the highest traditions of military service and reflect great credit on him, his unit, and the United States Army.

Distinguished Service Cross Citations

The Distinguished Service Cross was established by order of President Woodrow Wilson and was born as part of the new Pyramid Of Honor that was established during the 1917 review of Medal of Honor awards. Prior to establishment of the D.S.C. by virtue of War Department General Orders Number 6 of January 12, 1918, and by Act of Congress on July 9, 1918, the Medal of Honor was the only American award for valor in combat available to American servicemen.

The Distinguished Service Cross has been in effect since April 6, 1917; however, under certain circumstances the Distinguished Service Cross may be awarded for services rendered prior to April 6, 1917. It is the highest U.S. Army award that can be awarded to civilians in service to the military or to foreign nationals. Even in these cases, the criteria for award are the same.

An asterisk (*) indicates the medal was awarded posthumously.

AKAHOSHI, IRVING M.

Headquarters, Fifth U.S. Army,
General Orders No. 102 (June 18, 1944)
Home Town: Honolulu, Hawaii
Citation: The President of the United States takes pleasure in presenting the Distinguished Service Cross to Irving M. Akahoshi (30102373), Private First Class, U.S. Army, for extraordinary heroism in connection with military operations against an armed enemy as a member of the 442d Regimental Combat Team in action against enemy forces on 16 May 1944, near Cisterna, Italy. Private First Class Akahoshi voluntarily accompanied an officer on a patrol to secure information of enemy units and dispositions in a vital sector of the front. All previous patrols of combat strength had attempted without success to take prisoners in this well defended sector. Private First Class Akahoshi and the officer infiltrated approximately eight hundred yards through the enemy line to outposts. While observing enemy dispositions, he observed a strong enemy outpost situated in a small ditch. To reach this outpost, Private First Class Akahoshi and the officer, in broad daylight, crawled two hundred fifty yards across an open field, exposed to enemy observation from the German main line of resistance on the command slope to their rear. Arriving at a point near the outpost, they surprised two Germans armed with machine pistols who were acting as security. After aiding in the cap-

ture of these two prisoners, Private First Class Akahoshi retraced his perilous route and successfully by-passed two enemy listening posts to arrive at his own lines. Private First Class Akahoshi's daring accomplishment provided vital information and identification of enemy units in a critical sector of the front.

ARAO, HENRY Y.
Headquarters, Fifth U.S. Army,
General Orders No. 114 (July 9, 1944)
Home Town: Santa Cruz, California
Citation: The President of the United States takes pleasure in presenting the Distinguished Service Cross to Henry Y. Arao (19013919), Staff Sergeant, U.S. Army, for extraordinary heroism in connection with military operations against an armed enemy while serving with 442d Regimental Combat Team, in action against enemy forces on 5 April 1945 near Seravezza, Italy. In attacking an enemy hill strongpoint, two squads of an infantry company were halted by machine gun, rifle and grenade fire. The support squad, composed mainly of replacements with Staff Sergeant Arao (then Private First Class) as first scout, was ordered to outflank the defensive position. Leading the attack, Staff Sergeant Arao boldly crawled forward through heavily mined approaches under a shower of mortar and rifle grenade fire toward a machine gun emplacement. During the advance, a grenade burst wounded the squad leader, alarming and confusing the squad members. Calmly and efficiently administering first aid, Staff Sergeant Arao quickly restored the confidence of his inexperienced comrades. The enemy, making a frantic attempt to halt the advance, covered the area with grenades and inflicted several casualties. Undaunted by this furious onslaught, Staff Sergeant Arao crawled alone to within seven yards of the enemy gun. Rising quickly to his knees, he lobbed a grenade into the emplacement, followed with a burst from his sub-machine gun, charged the nest, killed the gunner and forced the assistant gunner to surrender. Fired upon by another machine gun, he flattened himself on the ground, inched his way toward the emplacement, tossed another grenade and then fired upon the crew with deadly accuracy. Demoralized, the rest of the enemy fled to a bomb-proof dugout. With the machine guns silenced and the enemy driven off by Staff Sergeant Arao's daring action, the platoon moved forward and effectively neutralized the dugout entrances. Staff Sergeant Arao's courage, driving energy and fearless determination to close with and destroy the enemy exemplify the spirit and traditions of the Infantry of the United States.

AWAKUNI, MASAO

Headquarters, Fifth U.S. Army,
General Orders No. 91 (May 27,1944)
Home Town: Hawaii
Citation: The President of the United States takes pleasure in presenting the Distinguished Service Cross to Masao Awakuni (30102030),
Private, U.S. Army, for extraordinary heroism in connection with
military operations against an armed enemy as a member of Company C, 100th Infantry Battalion, in action against enemy forces on
8 February 1944, near Cassino, Italy. While advancing in an attack,
Private Awakuni's company encountered an enemy tank upon which
was mounted a 75-mm. gun. The enemy tank immediately went into
action, supported by intense machine gun and sniper fire, forcing
the company to take cover. Rifle grenadiers failed to stop the firing
from the tank. Private Awakuni was called from the support platoon
to attempt to fire at the tank with his rocket launcher. He worked
his way across fifty yards of open ground and arrived at a point only
thirty yards from the hostile armor. Although he had poor protective
cover, Private Awakuni coolly took aim, and with his first shell hit
the tread of the tank. His second shell was a dud. Having disclosed
his position from the first two shots, Private Awakuni was subjected
to heavy enemy fire. Despite the deadly peril facing him, he calmly
took aim for a third time and made a direct hit on the tank, causing it
to burst into flames. Private Awakuni then sought the sparse protection of a nearby rock and was forced to remain in this position until
darkness permitted his return to friendly lines. For ten hours he was
pinned down by deadly sniper fire, and in his attempt to return to
his lines in darkness, he was wounded in the arm by machine gun
fire. His courage and tenacity in the face of deadly fire were an inspiration to his fellow soldiers and reflect the finest traditions of the
Armed forces of the United States.

FUJIWARA, YOSHIMI R.

Headquarters, Sixth Army Group,
General Orders No. 7 (January 29, 1945)
Home Town: Honolulu, Hawaii
Citation: The President of the United States takes pleasure in presenting the Distinguished Service Cross to Yoshimi R. Fujiwara
(30104334), Staff Sergeant, U.S. Army, for extraordinary heroism in
connection with military operations against an armed enemy while
serving with Company G, 442nd Regimental Combat Team, in action against enemy forces in the vicinity of Bruyères, France, on 20
October 1944. In attempting to flank an enemy strongpoint defended by three machine gun sections and other automatic weapons, the

platoon in which Staff Sergeant Fujiwara was a squad leader was pinned down and virtually surrounded in a long narrow strip of undergrowth which offered concealment but no cover. Having engaged the enemy in a fire fight, the platoon found itself further menaced by machine gun and shell fire from an approaching force of two Mark IV tanks, supported by two columns of fifty enemy troops. Realizing that drastic action was necessary to avert the complete annihilation of the platoon, Sergeant Fujiwara climbed a slight knoll in the area and attempted with anti-tank grenades to halt the tanks' progress. Finding that this fire was ineffective, he ordered the bazooka team to relinquish its weapon to him. Aware that the flash from the bazooka would reveal his position, he took deliberate aim at the leading tank and fired, scoring a partial hit. The tank, though temporarily slowed, continued its advance and raked his position with return fire from its machine gun. Racing against time and ignoring the enemy's awareness of his location, he continued to expose himself to the ever approaching tanks until he succeeded, with his fifth attempt, in putting one out of action. Upon seeing this, the second Mark IV rapidly withdrew, followed by its accompanying troops. Sergeant Fujiwara's fearlessness, cool-handed aggressiveness and consideration for the lives and safety of his comrades at the risk of his own life exemplify the highest traditions of the United States Army.

HIRATA, JESSE M.

Headquarters, Fifth U.S. Army,
General Orders No. 133 (August 8, 1944)
Home Town: Honolulu, Hawaii
Citation: The President of the United States takes pleasure in presenting the Distinguished Service Cross to Jesse M. Hirata (30102296), Private, U.S. Army, for extraordinary heroism in connection with military operations against an armed enemy as a member of Company B, 100th Infantry Battalion, in action against enemy forces on 5 June 1944, near Genzano, Italy. Private Hirata served as lead scout for his platoon during an advance. His unit halted for a short period of rest in an area where enemy snipers were extremely active. While reconnoitering the area, Private Hirata was fired upon by an enemy sniper. Hitting the ground, Private Hirata made his way toward the enemy position. In an attempt to fire at the enemy, Private Hirata's rifle failed to function. Unhesitatingly he picked up a German shovel lying nearby and charged into the German position, calling for assistance from his comrades. Seeing other soldiers coming to Private Hirata's assistance, three Germans surrendered to him. Private Hirata's heroic performance reflects the high standards of courage and initiative of the American Infantryman.

IIDA, GEORGE S.
Headquarters, Seventh U.S. Army,
General Orders No. 10 (January 16, 1945)
Home Town: Schofield Barracks, Hawaii
Citation: The President of the United States takes pleasure in presenting the Distinguished Service Cross to George S. Iida (30105499), Staff Sergeant, U.S. Army, for extraordinary heroism in connection with military operations against an armed enemy as a member of Company G, 442d Regimental Combat Team, in action against enemy forces on 4 July 1944, near Castellina, Italy. When his platoon was pinned down by fierce bursts of machine gun fire, Sergeant Iida, spotting two of the guns, successfully neutralized one machine gun emplacement with his M-1 rifle and directed the fire of his BAR man in silencing another. Reorganizing his men who had become scattered by the barrage, he advanced forward alone to reconnoiter the area. Encountering an enemy rifleman, he shot him at point blank range. This action caused the enemy to open up with intense machine gun and machine pistol fire. Locating one of these hostile positions, Sergeant Iida crawled to within a few yards of it and throwing two hand grenades, destroyed the machine gun nest. Meanwhile, his platoon leader was seriously wounded and Sergeant Iida was ordered to assume command of the platoon. Observing that the men were still held immobile by the concentrated enemy fire, he again advanced alone, located the hostile positions and heaved four more hand grenades into the emplacements, silencing the enemy weapons. By his fearless determination and outstanding bravery, Sergeant Iida successfully led his platoon in capturing their objective.

KIM, YOUNG OAK
Headquarters, Fifth U.S. Army,
General Orders No. 102 (1944)
Home Town: Los Angeles, California
Citation: The President of the United States takes pleasure in presenting the Distinguished Service Cross to Young O. Kim (0-1309572), First Lieutenant (Infantry), U.S. Army, for extraordinary heroism in connection with military operations against an armed enemy while serving with 100th Infantry Battalion, 442d Regimental Combat Team, in action against enemy forces near Cisterna, Italy, on 16 May 1944. First Lieutenant Kim, accompanied by one enlisted man, voluntarily went on a patrol to secure information of enemy units and dispositions in a vital sector of the front. All previous patrols of combat strength had attempted without success to take prisoners in this well defended sector. First Lieutenant Kim and his assistant infiltrated approximately 800 yards through the enemy line of outposts.

While observing enemy dispositions, he discovered a strong enemy outpost situated in a small ditch. To reach this outpost, First Lieutenant Kim and his assistant, in broad daylight, crawled 250 yards across an open field, exposed to enemy observation from the German main line of resistance on the commanding slope of their rear. Arriving at a point near the outpost, they surprised two Germans armed with machine pistols who were acting as security. By use of signs, First Lieutenant Kim warned the enemy to remain quiet. He retraced his perilous route with the two prisoners and successfully by-passed two enemy listening posts to arrive at his own lines. First Lieutenant Kim's courageous and daring performance provided vital information and identification of enemy units in a critical sector of the front.

*KODA, KIICHI

Headquarters, Fifth U.S. Army,
General Orders No. 153 (1944)
Home Town: Waipahu, Oahu, Hawaii
Citation: The President of the United States takes pride in presenting the Distinguished Service Cross (Posthumously) to Kiichi Koda (30101862), Private First Class, U.S. Army, for extraordinary heroism in connection with military operations against an armed enemy while serving with 100th Infantry Battalion, in action against enemy forces on 9 July 1944, near Castellina, Italy. Reaching a point fifty yards from its objective, Private First Class Koda's platoon received a volley of German machine gun and machine pistol fire from a wooded area. Private First Class Koda, accompanied by four comrades with fixed bayonets, charged into the woods. Firing their rifles from the hip whenever they spotted an enemy position, he and his comrades completely disrupted and disorganized the Germans in the area. Completing his mission, Private First Class Koda rejoined his squad which had been ordered to flank and guard a castle, the objective of an adjacent company. The enemy opened fire on the platoon with machine guns. Sensing the danger of a possible German attack, Private First Class Koda requested permission from his platoon leader to capture the castle. Instructing his comrades to cover his approach, he moved forward to a point five yards from the castle. Spotting an open window, he tossed a grenade into the building; then crept to each successive window, repeating the operation until he had completely circled the structure. Rejoining his squad, Private First Class Koda led his comrades, with fixed bayonets, into the castle. In the ensuing fight Private First Class Koda was mortally wounded by an enemy hand grenade; but as a result of his intrepid performance, three prisoners were captured, ten Germans killed,

and five machine guns and four machine pistols were taken. Private First Class Koda's fearless courage and fighting spirit were an inspiration to his fellow soldiers and serve as an example of the heroic traditions of the Army of the United States.

KURODA, HARUTO
Headquarters, Fifth U.S. Army,
General Orders No. 133 (August 3, 1944)
Home Town: Honolulu, Hawaii
Citation: The President of the United States takes pleasure in presenting the Distinguished Service Cross to Haruto Kuroda (30101838), Private First Class, U.S. Army, for extraordinary heroism in connection with military operations against an armed enemy as a member of Company B, 100th Infantry Battalion, in action against enemy forces on 2 June 1944, near La Torretto, Italy. Private First Class Kuroda's squad acted as point for the leading platoon in a daylight attack. Contacting an enemy machine gun nest, Private First Class Kuroda and two companions crawled two hundred yards through a wheat field toward the hostile weapon. Reaching a position ten yards from the machine gun, each man threw fragmentation grenades, killing three Germans. Another hostile position, containing two machine guns, opened fire on Private First Class Kuroda and his companions. Under intense fire he and his comrades crawled toward the second position. Nearing the enemy strongpoint, Private First Class Kuroda and his comrades opened fire with their rifles and threw hand grenades to kill two, wound one, and capture four Germans. Later in the day, when his platoon had reached its objective, an enemy machine gun opened fire on the units on the left flank. Again, Private First Class Kuroda and his two companions crawled toward the enemy, making their way through a vineyard to a point within ten feet of the Germans. Pinning the nest with rifle fire while one member of the squad tossed hand grenades, they boldly charged the position with fixed bayonets. Private First Class Kuroda and his fellow soldiers were successful in capturing eight Germans armed with two machine guns, three machine pistols and three rifles. In a period of approximately three hours, he and his companions neutralized five machine guns, five machine pistols, and killed or captured seventeen Germans. Private First Class Kuroda's aggressive and courageous actions exemplify the highest traditions of the Army of the United States.

*MADOKORO, HARRY F.

Headquarters, Fifth U.S. Army,
General Orders No. 175 (November 16, 1944)
Home Town: Poston, Arizona
Citation: The President of the United States takes pride in presenting the Distinguished Service Cross (Posthumously) to Harry F. Madokoro (31916617), Private First Class, U.S. Army, for extraordinary heroism in connection with military operations against an armed enemy while serving with Company K, 100th Infantry Battalion, in action against enemy forces on 7 July 1944 near Molino A Ventoabbto, and on 16 and 17 July 1944 in Luciana, Italy. During the final assault on an enemy held hill, Private First Class Madokoro advanced ahead of his squad to a strategic position from which he could deliver effective automatic rifle fire. Partly exposed to enemy fire, he scanned his sector of the slope for targets. He leveled his automatic rifle on a nest of snipers, forcing them to disperse. Throughout the bitter fight he held his position, neutralizing another enemy nest and paining down the enemy to enable his platoon to take the hill. Again at Luciana, Italy, Private First Class Madokoro occupied an advanced position and proceeded to fire on the enemy entrenched on the outskirts of the town. With heavy fire directed at him, he stubbornly held his position and provided covering fire when his squad was forced to withdraw because of a concentrated artillery and mortar barrage. The following day, when his squad became separated from the remainder of the company within the town, Private First Class Madokoro provided flank protection against determined enemy attacks. A group of enemy soldiers entered a nearby draw and threw hand grenades into the enemy position. On another occasion he left his position and silenced a machine pistol position with a grenade. Still later in the course of the battle, he approached an enemy machine gun nest and silenced it by firing from a kneeling position. By his stubborn determination, conspicuous devotion to duty and courage, Private First Class Madokoro inspired his squad in preventing the enemy's escape while his company closed in to occupy the town. His valorous performance is exemplary of the finest traditions of the Armed Forces of the United States.

*MASUDA, KAZUO

Headquarters, Fifth U.S. Army,
General Orders No. 95 (1945)
Home Town: Santa Ana, California
Citation: The President of the United States takes pride in presenting the Distinguished Service Cross (Posthumously) to Kazuo Masuda (39166362), Staff Sergeant, U.S. Army, for extraordinary hero-

ism in connection with military operations against an armed enemy while serving with 100th Infantry Battalion, in action against enemy forces on 6 July 1944, near Molino A Ventoabbto and from 27 to 28 August 1944, on the Arno River near Florence, Italy. On 6 July 1944, while his advanced observation post was the target of heavy mortar and artillery barrages, Staff Sergeant Masuda crawled two hundred yards to the mortar section, secured a mortar tube and ammunition and returned to the observation post. Using his helmet as a base-plate, Staff Sergeant Masuda single-handedly directed effective fire upon the enemy for twelve hours, inflicting heavy casualties and re-pulsing two major enemy counterattacks. On 27 August 1944, Staff Sergeant Masuda voluntarily led two men on a night patrol across the Arno River and through the heavily mined and booby-trapped north bank. Hearing movements to his right, he ordered his men to cover him while he crawled forward and discovered that a strong enemy force had surrounded them. Realizing that he was trapped, he ordered his men to withdraw while he boldly engaged two enemy automatic weapons. At the sacrifice of his life, he enabled his com-rades to escape with valuable information which materially aided the successful crossing of the Arno River. The gallant heroism and selfless devotion to duty of Staff Sergeant Masuda exemplify the fin-est traditions of the Infantry of the Army of the United States.

MIYAMOTO, FUJIO
Headquarters, Sixth Army Group,
General Orders No. 19 (March 27, 1945)
Home Town: Honolulu, Hawaii
Citation: The President of the United States takes pleasure in presenting the Distinguished Service Cross to Fujio Miyamoto (30105168), Staff Sergeant, U.S. Army, for extraordinary heroism in connection with military operations against an armed enemy while serving with Company K, 442d Regimental Combat Team, in action against enemy forces on 29 October 1944 near Biffontaine, France. When the forward elements of Sergeant Miyamoto's company were pinned down by fire from an enemy machine gun and supporting snipers, he fearlessly worked his way forward toward the enemy em-placement. While so engaged, he was wounded in the forearm by a sniper, but disdaining medical treatment, he continued to advance until he reached a point 25 yards from the emplacement. Expos-ing himself in order to get better observation, he opened fire with his sub-machine gun, killed the two gunners and thus neutralized the position. In the 2-hour fire fight which followed, Staff Sergeant Miyamoto accounted for five more of the enemy and refused to be evacuated until the initial objective was reached.

MIYASHIRO, TAKEICHI T.
Headquarters, Fifth U.S. Army,
General Orders No. 149 (September 7, 1944)
Home Town: Honokaa, Hawaii
Citation: The President of the United States takes pleasure in presenting the Distinguished Service Cross to Takeichi T. Miyashiro (0-10703701), Second Lieutenant, U.S. Army, for extraordinary heroism in connection with military operations against an armed enemy while serving with Company C, 100th Infantry Battalion, in action against enemy forces on 8 July 1944, near Castellina, Italy. In a dawn attack, Second Lieutenant Miyashiro led his platoon to take the company objective. Establishing a defensive position, Second Lieutenant Miyashiro took a squad to the right flank to eliminate a machine gun nest situated in a house. With constant sniper fire harassing the squad, he led his men in taking the house, killing one German and taking one prisoner. The enemy immediately launched a counterattack to drive the squad from the house. When the Germans had approached to points within thirty feet of the house, Second Lieutenant Miyashiro ordered his men to open fire and the enemy fled in disorder. Second Lieutenant Miyashiro then established an observation post in the house and posted local security. An hour later the enemy again attacked the building. Firing effectively with an M-1 Rifle, Second Lieutenant Miyashiro cut the enemy platoon to a squad and repulsed the assault. The Germans launched a third counterattack, supported by an 88-mm. barrage directed pointblank at the house. Refusing to withdraw, Second Lieutenant Miyashiro and a handful of men held their post. When .70- mm. shells began falling in the area, Second Lieutenant Miyashiro ordered his men to withdraw, while he remained at this post to obtain information of enemy activity. When the barrage lifted, he opened fire on the charging enemy, and with the aid of a machine gun on the left flank, succeeded in taking a heavy toll of the enemy to break up the attack. The courage, tenacity, and fighting determination displayed by Second Lieutenant Miyashiro provided an inspiration for his men, and his performance exemplifies the finest traditions of the Army of the United States.

*NAKASAKI, ROBERT K.
Headquarters, Fifth U.S. Army,
General Orders No. 110 (1945)
Home Town: Los Angeles, California
Citation: The President of the United States takes pride in presenting the Distinguished Service Cross (Posthumously) to Robert K. Nakasaki (39017321), Sergeant, U.S. Army, for extraordinary heroism

in connection with military operations against an armed enemy as a member of Company A, 100th Infantry Battalion, in action against enemy forces on 5 April 1945 near Servezza, Italy. Under cover of a brief artillery barrage, Sergeant Nakasaki's platoon advanced up the northern slope of Hill Georgia. As he and his men neared the summit, concentrated and intense fire from six machine guns, machine pistols and rifle fire forced the platoon to take cover. With complete disregard for personal safety, Sergeant Nakasaki grabbed his rifle, equipped with a grenade launcher, and crawled through a minefield to within fifteen yards of a well dug-in machine gun emplacement. Exposing himself to hostile fire, he launched a grenade at the nest and completely destroyed it. Quickly reloading his rifle, he fired and destroyed another machine gun on his right flank, killing two of the enemy. Before he could take cover, Sergeant Nakasaki was killed by the fire of an enemy sniper. Taking advantage of the gap thus created in the enemy defenses, the platoon quickly advanced and seized its objective. Sergeant Nakasaki's heroic action and fearlessness in the face of great danger were an inspiration to all and an everlasting tribute to the American Infantryman.

ONO, THOMAS Y.
Headquarters, Fifth U.S. Army,
General Orders No. 133 (August 3, 1944)
Home Town: Honolulu, Hawaii
Citation: The President of the United States takes pleasure in presenting the Distinguished Service Cross to Thomas Y. Ono (30105796), Private, U.S. Army, for extraordinary heroism in connection with military operations against an armed enemy while serving with Company B, 100th Infantry Battalion, in action against enemy forces on 2 June 1944, near La Torretto, Italy. Private Ono's squad acted as point for the leading platoon in a daylight attack. Contacting an enemy machine gun nest, Private Ono and two companions crawled two hundred yards through a wheat field toward the hostile weapon. Reaching a position ten yards from the machine gun, each man threw fragmentation grenades, killing three Germans. Another hostile position, containing two machine guns, opened fire on Private Ono and his companions. Under intense fire he and his comrades crawled toward the second position. Nearing the enemy strongpoint, Private Ono and his comrades opened fire with their rifles and threw hand grenades to kill two, wound one, and capture four Germans. Later in the day, when his platoon had reached its objective, an enemy machine gun opened fire on the units on the left flank. Again, Private Ono and his two companions crawled toward the enemy, making their way through a vineyard to a

point within ten feet of the Germans. Pinning the nest with rifle fire while one member of the squad tossed hand grenades, they boldly charged the position with fixed bayonets. Private Ono and his fellow soldiers were successful in capturing eight Germans armed with two machine guns, three machine pistols and three rifles. In a period of approximately three hours, he and his companions neutralized five machine guns, five machine pistols, and killed or captured seventeen Germans. Private Ono's aggressive and courageous actions exemplify the highest traditions of the Army of the United States.

*OTAKE, MASANAO

Headquarters, Sixth Army Group,
General Orders No. 13 (December 13, 1944)
Home Town: Lahaina, Maui, Hawaii
Citation: The President of the United States takes pride in presenting the Distinguished Service Cross (Posthumously) to Masanao Otake (0-1703069), Second Lieutenant, U.S. Army, for extraordinary heroism in connection with military operations against an armed enemy while serving with Company C, 100th Infantry Battalion, 442d Regimental Combat Team, in action against enemy forces on 17 October 1944, in the vicinity of Bruyères, France. In the 100th's attack on Hill 578, it became necessary to send some riflemen to an isolated farmhouse, situated on flat open ground, to secure the battalion's left flank. Lieutenant Otake, who was assigned the task of leading a squad of eight men to capture the enemy occupied farmhouse, dashed out toward the building, running through a hundred yards of open field raked by machine gun and small arms fire. Inspired by his example, his men immediately followed, and after a brief fire-fight succeeded in capturing the farmhouse. Observing that Lieutenant Otake and his men were in a vulnerable position, an enemy platoon launched a determined counter-attack against the farmhouse. Though greatly outnumbered, Lieutenant Otake urged his men to hold their hard-earned position, and while gallantly resisting the enemy assault he was mortally wounded by several machine pistol bullets and died a short while later. By complete disregard for his personal safety, gallant leadership and determination of purpose, Lieutenant Otake exemplified the finest traditions of the United States Army.

SUEHIRO, MASARU

Headquarters, Fifth U.S. Army,
General Orders No. 77 (1944)
Home Town: Honolulu, Hawaii
Citation: The President of the United States takes pleasure in presenting the Distinguished Service Cross to Masaru Suehiro

(30100039), Corporal, U.S. Army, for extraordinary heroism in connection with military operations against an armed enemy while serving with Company A, 100th Infantry Battalion, in action against enemy forces on 29 November 1943, near Cerasuolo, Italy. After taking its objective, Corporal Suehiro's company was subjected to an enemy counterattack supported by machine gun and mortar fire. Corporal Suehiro, leader of a 60-mm. mortar squad, moved forward in the face of intense enemy fire to an exposed position in order to direct his mortar fire. His position, although almost untenable because of heavy enemy mortar and machine gun fire, afforded excellent observation. From this hazardous observation post he directed accurate fire on an enemy machine gun, destroying the weapon and depriving the enemy of essential supporting fire. Observing an enemy group forming for an assault, he started to adjust his fire but was seriously wounded by shell fragments. Although suffering intense pain, he remained in his hazardous position and continued to direct such effective fire that the enemy counterattack was successfully repulsed. Corporal Suehiro's determined courage and steadfast devotion to duty contributed materially to the defense by his company, and his performance reflects the finest traditions of the Armed Forces.

*SUGIYAMA, TOGO S.

Headquarters, Fifth U.S. Army,
General Orders No. 153 (1944)
Home Town: Los Angeles, California
Citation: The President of the United States takes pride in presenting the Distinguished Service Cross (Posthumously) to Togo S. Sugiyama (39163051), Sergeant, U.S. Army, for extraordinary heroism in connection with military operations against an armed enemy while serving with Company H, 442d Regimental Combat Team, in action against enemy forces on 12 July 1944, near Pastina, Italy. To support a company attack, Sergeant Sugiyama emplaced his machine gun on the crest of a saddle between two hills so that his fire could cover the forward slope of both hills. Then, exposed to grazing small arms fire, he crawled along the ridge to a commanding position in order to direct fire. Locating an enemy machine gun and snipers on the left flank, Sergeant Sugiyama made his way along the reverse slope of the hill and reached a point directly opposite the enemy weapon. He killed two snipers with rifle fire and forced the machine gunners to withdraw. Returning to his observation post, he located a dugout occupied by two snipers who were firing on his machine gun position. Securing several grenades he led three riflemen in attacking the dugout to kill one German and force the other to surrender.

Later, Sergeant Sugiyama fired tracer bullets to designate a German machine gun position, to enable nearby riflemen to neutralize the weapon. After reporting to nearby riflemen the presence of enemy troops located in a concrete house, Sergeant Sugiyama observed two German machine gun squads approaching the forward slope of the left hill. Crawling to a position of better visibility, and exposing himself to enemy fire, Sergeant Sugiyama fired three rifle grenades to kill five Germans and force the remainder to flee. Another machine gun across the valley opened fire on him, but withdrew before he could return fire. As he started to crawl back to his squad, Sergeant Sugiyama was fired upon by a concealed machine gun. Rising to return fire, Sergeant Sugiyama was killed instantly. By his fearlessness, combat skill and initiative, Sergeant Sugiyama inflicted heavy casualties upon the enemy, and inspired his men by his intrepidity and self-sacrificing devotion to duty.

*TAKATA, SHIGEO JOSEPH
Headquarters, Fifth U.S. Army,
General Orders No. 94 (November 23, 1943)
Home Town: Oahu, Hawaii
Citation: The President of the United States takes pride in presenting the Distinguished Service Cross (Posthumously) to Shigeo Joseph Takata (30102426), Sergeant, U.S. Army, for extraordinary heroism in connection with military operations against an armed enemy while serving with Company B, 100th Infantry Battalion (Separate), in action against enemy forces on the morning of 9 September 1943, west of Monte Milleto, Italy. Sergeant Takata personally led his squad in a flanking movement, forcing the withdrawal of enemy machine gunners and materially assisting in the attainment of the Battalion objective. Taking position in front of his men, he led them through intense artillery, mortar and machine gun fire to carry out his mission. He continuously and deliberately disregarded his own welfare in making personal reconnaissance to determine enemy gun positions. While so exposing himself, he was struck by an artillery shell and mortally wounded. In spite of his wounds he attempted to communicate with his platoon leader to inform him what he had learned of the enemy positions. His courage and devotion to duty were an inspiration to the members of his unit and reflect high credit upon himself and the military service.

TAKEMOTO, TSUNEO
Headquarters, Sixth Army Group,
General Orders No. 5 (January 26, 1945)
Citation: The President of the United States takes pleasure in present-

ing the Distinguished Service Cross to Tsuneo Takemoto (30103873), Technical Sergeant, U.S. Army, for extraordinary heroism in connection with military operations against an armed enemy while a member of Company E, 442d Regimental Combat Team, in action against enemy forces on 29 October 19454 in the vicinity of Biffontaine, France. In completing the capture of Hill 617, Sergeant Takemoto's platoon spearheaded the attack of his company. When his platoon was pinned down by a well dug-in enemy armed with automatic weapons, he ran a distance of 30 yards directly into the face of enemy fire, raking the enemy positions with his Thompson sub-machine gun. As he ran he shouted to draw hostile fire, making the enemy troops reveal their exact locations to his men. Inspired by his fearless action, his comrades charged after him and destroyed the strong-point. When his platoon was counter-attacked by twelve enemy troops supported by four automatic weapons, he organized his men into a skirmish line that checked the initial rush. Then, sending out a flanking party whose fire temporarily confused the enemy, he led his men in a charge against the attackers. Once again he ran a distance of thirty yards into the face of hostile fire shouting to attract enemy fire to himself and giving his charging men the opportunity to advance with a minimum of risk. Inspired by his fearlessness, his men completely routed the enemy, and during the action captured 34 prisoners. By his fearlessness and skillful leadership, Sergeant Takemoto won the respect and confidence of his men, and reflects great honor upon the armed forces of the United States.

*TANIMOTO, LARRY T.

Headquarters, European Theater of Operations, U.S. Army,
General Orders No. 65 (1945)
Home Town: Honolulu, Hawaii
Citation: The President of the United States takes pride in presenting the Distinguished Service Cross (Posthumously) to Larry T. Tanimoto (30105535), Sergeant, U.S. Army, for extraordinary heroism in connection with military operations against an armed enemy as an acting platoon leader, Company I, 442d Regimental Combat Team, on 29 and 31 October 1944 and 3 November 1944, in the Vosges Mountains, France. Sergeant Tanimoto, while participating in an attack on "Suicide Hill", forced the surrender of two enemy gunners while making himself the sole target for another machine gun fifty yards away. He successfully led a heavily armed patrol in dispersing a numerically superior enemy mine-laying detail. While leading another patrol, an enemy machine gun wounded the scout and pinned the remaining men to the ground. Sergeant Tanimoto rose to his feet and killed two of the gun crew, giving his men an opportunity to

outflank the nest. The heroic courage and loyalty displayed by Sergeant Tanimoto in the face of great danger were in keeping with the highest military traditions.

TAZOI, JIM Y.
Headquarters, Fifth U.S. Army,
General Orders No. 52 (1945)
Home Town: Garland, Utah
Citation: The President of the United States takes pleasure in presenting the Distinguished Service Cross to Jim Y. Tazoi (20924666), Private First Class, U.S. Army, for extraordinary heroism in connection with military operations against an armed enemy as a member of Company K, 442d Regimental Combat Team, in action against enemy forces on 28 and 29 October, near Biffontaine, France. While serving as radioman for a command group, Private First Class Tazoi observed a concealed machine gun position which had been bypassed by forward elements. As the machine gunner attempted to fire at the command group, Private First Class Tazoi shouted warning to his comrades and opened fire on the nest to kill the gunner. The following day, Private First Class Tazoi, transporting his radio, joined the attacking elements in an advance under heavy automatic fire to take an enemy strongpoint. Later, he accompanied a group of riflemen in a bayonet charge against a strongly defended enemy hill position. Sighting an enemy machine gun nest, he exposed himself to heavy enemy fire and fired at the position to neutralize the effectiveness of the German weapon while his comrades assaulted the strongpoint. Although handicapped by his radio which made him an easier target for the hostile fire directed at him, he rushed to the assistance of two comrades who were trapped by two Germans throwing grenades. Struck by a sniper's bullet, he determinedly continued to advance and reached a clear field of fire. As he killed the two German grenade throwers he was wounded a second time by grenade fragments. The prodigious courage and fighting spirit of Private First Class Tazoi bring honor to the Armed Forces of the United States.

*YAMANAGA, THOMAS I.
Headquarters, Fifth U.S. Army,
General Orders No. 37 (March 9, 1944)
Home Town: Hawaii
Citation: The President of the United States takes pride in presenting the Distinguished Service Cross (Posthumously) to Thomas I. Yamanaga (30102445), Private First Class, U.S. Army, for extraordinary heroism in connection with military operations against an

armed enemy while serving with Company A, 100th Infantry Battalion (Separate), in action against enemy forces on 21 October 1943, in the vicinity of Alife, Italy. While attacking enemy positions, the company in which Private First Class Yamanaga was a gunner was pinned down by heavy enemy machine gun fire from the front. On his own initiative, Private First Class Yamanaga worked his way forward in full view of the enemy, to a position where he could engage the enemy gun with his automatic rifle. He immediately delivered such effective fire that the enemy gun was silenced, whereupon his company, no longer pinned down, successfully continued the attack. Private First Class Yamanaga was mortally wounded in rendering this outstanding service to his fellow soldiers. His initiative and courage in the face of danger were an inspiration to all who witnessed his bold deed.

*YAMASHIRO, GORDON
Headquarters, Sixth Army Group,
General Orders No. 18 (March 24, 1945)
Home Town: Honolulu, Hawaii
Citation: The President of the United States takes pride in presenting the Distinguished Service Cross (Posthumously) to Gordon Yamashiro (30105540), Staff Sergeant, U.S. Army, for extraordinary heroism in connection with military operations against an armed enemy while serving with Company K, 442d Regimental Combat Team, in action against enemy forces on 28 October 1944 near Biffontaine, France. Sergeant Yamashiro's company was advancing against dominating enemy positions when it was suddenly pinned down by the crossfire of two machine guns supported by riflemen and grenadiers. Immediately sizing up the dangerous situation, he deployed his squad to cover his movements and advanced alone to espy the enemy positions. After determining the probable source of the enemy fire he advanced 100 yards, killed a sniper who fired at him and missed, then neutralized with BAR fire one of the gun positions by killing three of its crew members. Continuing his audacious movements under fire from the second gun position, he killed the two gunners, thus neutralizing the emplacement. While engaged in laying down a protective screen of fire for his company's subsequent advance Sergeant Yamashiro was fatally shot by an enemy sniper.

YASUTAKE, ROBERT R.
Headquarters, Fifth U.S. Army,
General Orders No. 133 (August 8, 1944)
Home Town: Lahaina, Maui, Hawaii
Citation: The President of the United States takes pleasure in present-

ing the Distinguished Service Cross to Robert R. Yasutake, Private First Class, U.S. Army, for extraordinary heroism in connection with military operations against an armed enemy while serving with Company C, 100th Infantry Battalion, in action against enemy forces near Lanuvio, Italy, on 2 June 1944. Private First Class Yasutake served as automatic rifleman for his squad during an attack. When his squad and the unit to his right became pinned down by heavy fire, he crawled to a position from which he opened fire and neutralized a hostile machine gun nest. Sensing an enemy machine gun fire coming from a deep gully, Private First Class Yasutake moved to the edge of the ravine, located the enemy position, and engaged the hostile crew with his automatic rifle and grenades, wounding seven Germans. As the fighting continued, his platoon encountered a series of enemy dugouts. Private First Class Yasutake, taking a position in one of the captured dugouts, engaged an enemy dugout fifteen yards from his own. The enemy threw hand grenades at him and attempted to infiltrate his position. Aware of the danger of being surrounded, he remained on the alert and killed a German who attempted to crawl toward him through a grape vineyard. Later, he spotted three Germans advancing in an attempt to isolate him from his platoon. When the Germans were within twenty yards of his dugout, he opened fire with his automatic rifle, killing them. Private First Class Yasutake's heroic and determined stand made it possible for his platoon to come abreast of him and continue the attack. His performance reflects the finest traditions of the Armed Forces of the United States.

*YOGI, MATSUICHI
Headquarters, European Theater of Operations, U.S. Army, General Orders No. 45 (March 25, 1945)
Home Town: Hawaii
Citation: The President of the United States takes pride in presenting the Distinguished Service Cross (Posthumously) to Matsuichi Yogi (30104464), Private First Class, U.S. Army, for extraordinary heroism in connection with military operations against an armed enemy while serving with Company K, 442d Regimental Combat Team, in action against enemy forces in the Vosges Mountains, France, from 27 October 1944 to 29 October 1944. Private First Class Yogi, during an enemy counterattack, daringly exposed himself and with his bazooka knocked out a German Mark IV tank. Disregarding enemy sniper fire, he eliminated one of two German bazookas with his own weapon and knocked out the other one with accurate rifle fire. On the second day, he scored a near hit on an enemy machine gun post which enabled his platoon to overrun the position. Private First Class Yogi's fighting spirit and intrepid gallantry above and beyond the call of duty, add living glory to the highest traditions of the Armed Forces.

YOKOTA, YUKIO

Headquarters, Fifth U.S. Army,
General Orders No. 133 (August 3, 1944)
Home Town: Honolulu, Hawaii
Citation: The President of the United States takes pleasure in presenting the Distinguished Service Cross to Yukio Yokota (30100987), Staff Sergeant, U.S. Army, for extraordinary heroism in connection with military operations against an armed enemy as a member of Company B, 100th Infantry Battalion, in action against enemy forces on 2 June 1944, near La Torretto, Italy. Staff Sergeant Yokota's squad acted as point for the leading platoon in a daylight attack. Contacting an enemy machine gun nest, Staff Sergeant Yokota and two companions crawled two hundred yards through a wheat field toward the hostile weapon. Reaching a position ten yards from the machine gun, each man threw fragmentation grenades, killing three Germans. Another hostile position, containing two machine guns, opened fire on Staff Sergeant Yokota and his companions. Under intense fire he and his comrades crawled toward the second position. Nearing the enemy strongpoint, Staff Sergeant Yokota and his comrades opened fire with their rifles and threw hand grenades to kill two, wound one, and capture four Germans. Later in the day, when his platoon had reached its objective, an enemy machine gun opened fire on the units on the left flank. Again, Staff Sergeant Yokota and his two companions crawled toward the enemy, making their way through a vineyard to a point within ten feet of the Germans. Pinning the nest with rifle fire while one member of the squad tossed hand grenades, they boldly charged the position with fixed bayonets. Staff Sergeant Yokota and his fellow soldiers were successful in capturing eight Germans armed with two machine guns, three machine pistols and three rifles. In a period of approximately three hours, he and his companions neutralized five machine guns, five machine pistols, and killed or captured seventeen Germans. Staff Sergeant Yokota's aggressive and courageous actions exemplify the highest traditions of the Army of the United States.

Killed In Action

The following is a listing of those Nisei warriors who were killed during World War II. Sorted by name, each field contains name, Unit/Company/Class, and hometown, if available.

ABE,Chester K.,442-M,Sacramento ,CA
AJITOMI,Matsuei,100-C,Lahaina ,HI
AJITOMI,Tokio,100-C,Lahaina ,HI
AKIMOTO,John,100-C,Los Angeles ,CA
AKIMOTO,Victor,100-A,Los Angeles ,CA
AKIYAMA,Zentaro G.,442-F,Sacramento ,CA
AKIYAMA,Hideo,100-C,Eleele ,HI
AMABE,Eugene T.,MIS,Spokane ,WA
AMAKAWA,Nobuo,442-I,Honolulu ,HI
ANDERSON,Daniel J.,100-B,Queens Co ,NY
ANZAI,James H.,442-F,Waipahu ,HI
AOYAMA,Yoshiharu N.,442-Can,Los Angeles ,CA
ARAKAKI,William H.,Army Unit,Kahaluu ,HI
ARAKAWA,Harold Jentoku,100-A,Puuene ,HI
ARAKAWA,James Yasushi,442-F,Honolulu ,HI
ARAKI,Masashi,100-C,Selma ,CA
ARIKAWA,Frank N.,442-F,Los Angeles ,CA
ARITA,Hiroaki,100-B,Paauilo ,HI
ASADA,Tatsumi,Army Unit,Puuene ,HI
ASAHINA,Shiro,305th-Inf,Salt Lake City ,UT
ASAI,Ralph Yukio,100-B,HI
ASATO,Shotaro Harry,232Eng,Hamakuapoko ,HI
ASAUMI,Kenneth Iwao,442-E,Honolulu ,HI
ASHIKAWA,Shigeo,100-A,Honolulu ,HI
BETSUI,Daniel Den,232Eng,Kauai ,HI
BOODRY,James,100-E/F,Clinton ,MA
BURT,Howard Vernon,442-K,
BYRNE,Joseph Lawrence,442-I,New York ,NY
CHIBANA,Henry Matsuzo,442-G,Koloa ,HI
CHINEN,Giichi,442-E,Haiku ,HI
CHINEN,Jenhatsu,442-E,Helemano ,HI
CHINEN,Onso,100-A,Koloa ,HI
CHORIKI,Danny Kiyoshi,232Eng,Makaweli,HI
CONNER,Cloudy Gray,100-D,Darlington Co ,SC
CRONE,Walter M.,442-H,Baltimore ,MD
DOI,Haruo,100-A,Honolulu ,HI
EATON,Kenneth E.,100-C,Penn ,OR

EBATA,Tetsu Ted,100-A,Koloa ,HI
EJI,William K.,349th-Inf,Honolulu ,HI
EKI,George,100-Hq,Honolulu ,HI
ENDO,Hiroo H.,442-G,Downey ,CA
ENDO,Masaharu,442-L,Honolulu ,HI
ENDO,Robert T.,442-K,Seattle ,WA
ENOMOTO,Kaname,442-G,Waipahu ,HI
ENOMOTO,Kiyozo,100-B,Aiea ,HI
ENSMINGER,Ralph B.,442-2Hq,Honolulu ,HI
ETHRIDGE,Harold C.,100-C,Uniontown ,AL
FARNUM JR,Charles O.,442-2Hq,Orangeburg ,SC
FRITZMEIER,Fred H.,442-L,WI
FUJI,Abe M.,232Eng,Salinas ,CA
FUJII,Masao,442-G,Honolulu ,HI
FUJII,Richard Toshio,100-B,Kealakekua ,HI
FUJII,Yutaka,100-C,Lihue ,HI
FUJIKAWA,Jitsuro,442-H,Hilo ,HI
FUJIKAWA,Masaki,442-E,Makalapa ,HI
FUJIKI,Charles S.,100-C,Salinas ,CA
FUJIKI,Hideo,522-Hq,Honolulu ,HI
FUJIMOTO,Toshiaki,100-D,Koloa ,HI
FUJINAKA,Noboru,442-L,Honolulu ,HI
FUJINO,Russell,MIS,San Francisco ,CA
FUJINO,Yoshimi,442-A.T,Hilo ,Hi
FUJINO,Yasuo P.,442-L,Seattle ,WA
FUJIOKA,Ted Teruo,442-A.T,Los Angeles ,CA
FUJIOKA,Teruo,442-L,Kahaluu ,HI
FUJIOKA,Wendell Shisuke,442-K,Pahala ,HI
FUJITA,Sadami,100-B,Aiea ,HI
FUJITANI,Ross K.,100-C,Kealakekua ,HI
FUJIWARA,Peter,Army Unit,Seattle ,WA
FUJIYAMA,Takeo,100-A,Lahaina ,HI
FUKAGAWA,Masami,100-Hq,Honolulu ,HI
FUKEDA,Akira Wallace,442-I,Puuene ,HI
FUKUBA,Shigeo Frank,442-F,Olaa ,HI
FUKUHARA,Herbert Masuo,100-A,Honolulu ,HI
FUKUI,Edwin Y.,MIS,Tacoma ,WA

FUKUMOTO,Roy Shizuo,100-C,Kohala ,HI
FUKUMURA,Ichiji,442-E,Lihue ,HI
FUKUNAGA,Chester T,100-F,Kukuihaele ,HI
FUKUOKA,Arthur M.,442-M,Los Angeles ,CA
FUKUSHIMA,Katsumi,442-G,Hilo ,HI
FUKUYAMA,Kaoru,100-D,Kohala ,HI
FUNAI,Stanley Kazuto,100-A,Kawailoa ,HI
FURUKAWA,Tatsumi,100-A,Concord ,CA
FURUKAWA,Tsuyoshi,100-A,Honolulu ,HI
FURUKAWA,Satoshi,100-B,Waikapu ,HI
FURUKIDO,Kenneth Kenzo,100-B,Honolulu ,HI
FURUSHIRO,Henry T.,100-B,Caldwell ,ID
FURUUCHI,Mitsuo,442-L,Papaikou ,HI
FUTAMATA,George M.,442-E,
FUYUMURO,Edward Shigeto,100-D,Aiea ,HI
GAGNON,Roland Joseph,442-E,
GANEKO,Seikichi,442-I,Kapaa ,HI
GODA,Hiroshi,100-Hq,Hilo ,HI
GOSHIKOMA,Ralph M.. 44-08,Waialua ,HI
GOYA,Kazuo,442-G,Waiakeauka ,HI
GOYA,Yeiko,100-C,Koloa ,HI
GUSHIKEN,George,442-L,Los Angeles ,CA
HACHIYA,Frank T. ,S. 42-12,Hood River ,OR
HADA,Victor K.,442-K,Denver ,CO
HADANO,Hatsuji,442-2Hq,Puuene ,HI
HAITA,Eiichi F.,442-I,Ione ,WA
HAJI,Tom S.,442-F,Spokane ,WA
HAMADA,Tetsuo,442-Can,Puunene ,HI
HAMAMOTO,Katsyoshi,442Med,Paia ,HI
HAMAMOTO,Seiichi,100-C,Waimanalo ,HI
ICHIKI,Stanley T.,302FaBn,Stockton ,CA
ICHIMURA,Kenichi,100-A,Honolulu ,HI
IDE,Edward Y.,100-Hq,Kaneohe ,HI
IGARASHI,Shigeo,100-B,Waialua ,HI
IGUCHI,Kiyoshi,442-F,Waipio ,HI
IHA,Masao,232Eng,Kapaa ,HI
IHARA,Kazuo,100-A,Hilo ,HI
IIDA,Martin M.,442-L,Kilauea ,HI
IIDA,George U.,442-E,Seattle ,WA
IKEDA,Katsumi,Army Unit,
IKEDA,Roy Y.,100-C,San Francisco ,CA
IKEDA,George T.,442-I,Holualoa ,HI
IKEDA,George T.,Snelling 45-09,Waialua ,HI
IKEDA,Isamu,100-Md,Ninole ,HI

IKEDA,William Y.,100-B,Paia ,HI
IKEDA,Masao,442-L,Seattle ,WA
IKEFUGI,Lloyd,442-F,Staten Island ,NY
IKEHARA,Henry S.,100-C,Wahiawa ,HI
IKEHARA,Kikuichiro,442-F,Wahiawa ,HI
IKEMOTO,Haruyuki,S. 43-07,Hamakuapoko ,HI
IKEMOTO,Kanemae,Army Unit,Waipouli ,HI
IKENO,James S.,100-D,Captain Cook ,HI
IMAI,Saburo,Army Unit,
IMAI,Sadao,Army Unit,
IMAI,Tomio,100-C,Haina ,HI
IMAMOTO,William I.,442Med,Tacoma ,WA
IMAMURA,Larry M.,100-B,Kekaha ,HI
IMANO,Susumu,Snelling 45-11,Kainalu ,HI
IMOTO,Shunichi B,Savage 43-07,Harding ,WA
INADA,Thomas T.,442-L,Honolulu ,HI
INAKAZU,Ben M.,442-I,Honolulu ,HI
INAMINE,Seiji,Army Unit,Halaula ,HI
INATSU,Masami,100-B,Seattle ,WA
INKYO,Suechi,Army Unit,Niulii ,HI
INOUE,Minoru,100-B,Honolulu ,HI
INOUYE,Eugene N.,Army Unit,
INOUYE,Tsutomu H.,Army Unit,
INOUYE,Itsutomu,Army Unit,Alameda ,CA
INOUYE,Kazuyoshi,Savage 43-07,Lihue ,HI
INOUYE,Masato,100-A,Honohina ,HI
IRIE,Masaji,100-C,Ewa ,HI
IRIGUCHI,Tadayoshi,442-E,Mahukona ,HI
ISERI,Mitsuo M.,100-D,Kent ,WA
ISHIDA,Minoru,442-G,San Marino ,CA
ISHIDA,Haruo,442-G,Seattle ,WA
ISHII,George F.,100-D,Eleele ,HI
ISHII,Masayuki,Snelling 45-09,Hilo ,HI
ISHII,Richard H.,100-C,Honolulu ,HI
ISHIKI,Walter S.,100-C,Honolulu ,HI
ISOBE,Kosaku,442Med,Haleiwa ,HI
ITO,Takashi,442-I,Denver ,CO
ITO,Hachiro,100-B,Honolulu ,HI
ITO,Tetsuo,442-G,Honolulu ,HI
IWAHIRO,Robert K.,442-A.T,Waipahu ,HI
IWAI,Hisashi,100-C,White River ,WA
IWAMASA,Yoshio,442-I,Niulii ,HI
IWAMOTO,Lawrence T.,100-Hq,Kaianaliu ,HI
IZUMIZAKI,Henry S.,442-F,Watsonville ,CA

JICHAKU,Thomas M.,442-G,Kapaa ,HI
JINNOHARA,Katsui,100-E,Paia ,HI
JOHNSON Jr.,John A,100-Hq,Honolulu ,HI
KADOOKA,Walter C.,100-F,Honaunau ,HI
Kadoyama,Joe Yazuru,Snelling 44-08,Kent ,WA
KAGAWA,Yasuo,100-E,Ewa ,HI
KAGIHARA,James J.,442-3Hq,Honolulu ,HI
KAIURA,Richard K.,Army Unit,Honolulu ,HI
KAJIKAWA,Tsugito,442-M,Kohala ,HI
KAJIWARA,Nobuo,100-B,Oakland ,CA
KAMEDA,Fred Y.,442-I,Waialua ,HI
KAMEOKA,Bob T.,442-F,Hanford ,CA
KAMETANI,Shinobu,442-G,Waikoa Kula ,HI
KAMI,Mitsuo,442-2Hq,Hilo ,HI
KAMIKAWA,Shizuto,442-3Hq,Honokaa ,HI
KANADA,James S.,100-A,Concord ,CA
KANAYA,Walter E.,442-2Hq,Helemano ,HI
KANAZAWA,John S.,442-K,Seattle ,WA
KANDA,Frank T.,442-M,Los Angeles ,CA
KANDA,Takezo,442-3Hq,Honolulu ,HI
KANEICHI,Takeo,442-E,Fresno. ,CA
KANEMITSU,Katsuhiro,442-M,Wailuku ,HI
KANESHIRO,Seichi,442-H,Kapoho ,HI
KANESHIRO,Yasuo,100-B,Makawao ,HI
KANETANI,Isamu,100-F,Hilo ,HI
KANETOMI,Jero,442-G,Kirkland ,WA
KANZAKI,Akira,442-E,Seattle ,WA
KARATSU,James S.,442-H,Los Angeles ,CA
KARIMOTO,Haruo,442-E,Kokoiki ,HI
KASHIWAEDA,Kenneth G.,442-L,Honolulu ,HI
KASHIWAGI,Kazuo,MIS,Los Angeles ,CA
KATAOKA,Yoshitaka,MIS,Kamaee ,HI
KATAYAMA,Noritada,442-E,Waikapu ,HI
KATO,John J,MIS,San Francisco ,CA
KATO,Joseph H.,442-E,Warm Springs ,CA
KATO,Kenji,442-M,Kohala ,HI
KATO,Yoshio,442-M,Seattle ,WA
KATSUDA,Masaichi C.,100-Md,Makaweli ,HI
KAWAGUCHI,John R.,442-L,Seattle ,WA
KAWAHARA,Richard H.,442-L,Makawao ,HI
KAWAKAMI,Tetsuro,442-G,Wailuku ,HI
KAWAMOTO,Haruo,442-F,Fresno. ,CA
KAWAMOTO,Haruo,100-A,Kailua ,HI
KAWAMOTO,Sadao,442-E,Lahaina ,HI

KAWAMOTO,Toshio,100-B,Honolulu ,HI
KAWAMOTO,Yutaka,100-B,Mountain View ,HI
KAWANISHI,Kikumatsu F.,100-F,Puueo ,HI
KAWANO,George U.,442-G,Denver ,CO
KAWANO,Tetsuo,100-E,Honolulu ,HI
KAWANO,Yasuo,100-D,Hilo ,HI
KAWANO,Cike C.,442-E,Powell ,WY
KAWATA,Albert G.,100-A,Honolulu ,HI
KAYA,Satoshi,100-C,Ewa ,HI
KAYA,Stephen M.,100-A,Honolulu ,HI
KENMOTSU,Yasuo,442-L,El Monte ,CA
KEY,Lewis A.,100-A,Trousdale Co ,TN
KIJIMA,Tadashi,442-2Hq,Pauwela-Maui,HI
KIKUCHI,Leo T.,442-G,Sebastopol ,CA
KIMURA,John E.,168th Inf,
KIMURA,John S.,MIS,Woodland ,CA
KIMURA,Paul T.,10thMtn,Los Angeles ,CA
KIMURA,Matsuichi,442-G,Honolulu ,HI
KIMURA,Paul Jr.,100-C,Wailuku ,HI
KIMURA,Tsuguo,442-2Hq,Hilo ,HI
KINA,Shomatsu E.,100-C,Paia ,HI
KINOSHITA,Mamoru,442-3Hq,Winton ,CA
KINOSHITA,Richard K.,100-E,Honolulu ,HI
KINOSHITA,Francis T.,100-C,Seattle ,WA
KIRITO,Toshio,442-F,Pahala ,HI
KISHI,Robert T.,442-G,Stockton (SLCity) ,CA
KITAGAWA,Roy J.,442-E,
KITSUE,Paul T.,442-F,Los Angeles ,CA
KIYABU,Ronald S.,100-A,Ookala ,HI
KIYOTA,Edward Y.,100-B,Honolulu ,HI
KODA,Kiichi,100-A,Waipahu ,HI
KOHARA,Sadaichi,442-K,Honolulu ,HI
KOITO,Sadamu,442-K,Wailuku ,HI
KOIZUMI,Yutaka,100-A,San Francisco ,CA
KOIZUMI,Hayato,100-B,Honolulu ,HI
KOJAKU,Shaw,442-F,Gardena ,CA
KOJIMA,Tadashi,442-L,Papaikou ,HI
KOKAME,Nobuo,442-F,Makaweli ,HI
KOKUBU,Jimmie T.,442-G,Portland ,OR
KOMATSU,James K.,100-B,Honolulu ,HI
KOMATSU,Katsuto,100-Hq,Hilo ,HI
KOMEDA,Fred H.,100-C,Honolulu ,HI
KOMOTO,Nobuo,442-E,Selma ,CA
KONDO,Henry M.,442-E,Pasadena ,CA

KONDO,Harushi,100-Hq,Aiea ,HI
KONDO,Herbert Y.,442-G,Hanapepe-Kauai ,HI
KONDOW,Howard N.,442-F,
KOTSUBO,Seichi,232Eng,Kapulena ,HI
KOYAMA,Isawo,Army Unit,Chewelah ,WA
KUBA,Shigeo,442-L,Honokaa ,HI
KUBO,Tadashi,442Med,Puuene ,HI
KUBO,Yoshio,100-A,Honolulu ,HI
KUBOKAWA,James K.,100-Hq,Honolulu ,HI
KUBOYAMA,Mitsuharu,442Med,Wahiawa ,HI
KUGE,Thomas T.,442-K,Portland ,OR
KUNIMATSU,Isamu,442-H,Anacortes ,WA
KURAOKA,Jerry S.,100-A,Wailuku ,HI
KURATA,Minoru,442-G,Haina ,HI
KURODA,Ichiji H.,100-E,Hakalau ,HI
KURODA (MH),Robert T.,442-H,Aiea ,HI
KUROKAWA,Satoshi B.,Snelling 44-08,Guadalupe ,CA
KUTAKA,Shosei,Army Unit,Puuene ,HI
KUTARA,Masaji,100-B,Honolulu ,HI
KUWADA,Joseph T. ,Savage 44-02,Honolulu ,Hi
KUWAHARA,Sunao,100-C,Wainaku ,HI
KYONO,John H.,442-F,Hood River ,OR
LAFFIN,William,Savage 42-12,Detroit ,MI
LANG,Clarence E.,442-3Hq,Canton ,OH
LUNA,Hideo Leonard,442-2Hq,Hilo ,HI
MADOKORO,Harry F.,442-K,Watsonville ,CA
MAEHARA,Saburo,100-C,Puuene ,HI
MAGARIFUJI,Richard K.,100-C,Kailua ,HI
MAKISHI,Matsutada,100-F,Makaweli ,HI
MANA,Seiso J.,100-E,Honolulu ,HI
MASAOKA,Ben F.,442-E,
MASAOKA,Kay K.,442-F,Lodi ,CA
MASHITA,Masatomo,100-A,Honolulu ,HI
MASUDA,Dick Z.,442-F,Stockton ,CA
MASUDA,Eso,442-F,Artesia ,CA
MASUDA,Kazuo,442-F,Santa Ana ,CA
MASUDA,Yoshito,100-C,Waiakoa ,HI
MASUMOTO,George H.,442-E,Selma ,CA
MASUMOTO,Noriyuki,232Eng,Kaumana ,HI
MASUMURA,Lawrence K.,100-A,Lihue ,HI
MASUNAGA,Kiyoshi,100-B,Hookena ,HI
MASUOKA,Peter S.,442-2Hq,Sebastopol ,CA
MATOBA,Michi,Army Unit,Portland ,OR
MATSUDA,Carl G.,442-I,Honaunau ,HI

MATSUI,Masao,100-C,Spreckelsville ,HI
MATSUKAWA,Hiroshi,100-A,Hilo ,HI
MATSUKAWA,Isamie,442-G,Salt Lake City ,UT
MATSUMOTO,Dick Y.,232Eng,Honolulu ,HI
MATSUMOTO,Goro,442-I,Honolulu ,HI
MATSUMOTO,Kiyuichi,442-Can,Papaikou ,HI
MATSUMOTO,Sadao,100-C,Olaa ,HI
MATSUMOTO,Tomio T.,100-F,Hilo ,HI
MATSUMURA,Renkichi,442-E,Hilo ,HI
MATSUNAGA,Kaname,100-A,Kalaheo ,HI
MATSUOKA,Satoshi,100-B,Honohina ,HI
MATSUSHIMA,Kazuo,100-B,Waimea ,HI
MATSUSHITA,Shizuo J.,442-K,Maulua ,HI
MAYEDA,George M.,100-C,Kelso ,WA
MEKATA,Thomas T.,100-D,Waipahu ,HI
MIGITA,Torao,Army Unit,Kalihiwai ,HI
MIHO,Katsuaki,442Med,Honolulu ,HI
MINAMI,Yoshio T.,100-Hq,Kapaa ,HI
MINATODANI,Isamu,442-I,Honolulu ,HI
MINE,Kiyoshi,Army Unit,Los Angeles ,CA
MISUMI,Tom T.,442-F,Oakland ,CA
MITANI,Kazuo,442-F,Salt Lake City ,UT
MITO,Kazuo,100-A,Honolulu ,HI
MIURA,Toshio,100-A,Waipahu ,HI
MIURA,Jack E.,1399Eng,Puhi ,HI
MIURA,Larry N.,442-K,Ewa ,HI
MIURA,Toshio,Snelling 45-05,Waipahu ,HI
MIYABE,Charles M.,100-A,Honolulu ,HI
MIYAGI,Masayoshi,100-E,Aiea ,HI
MIYAGUCHI,Masayuki J.,442-H,Ewa ,HI
MIYAKE,Tetsuo,100-B,Eleele ,HI
MIYAMOTO,James H.,442-K,Pepeekeo ,HI
MIYAMOTO,Thomas T.,100-C,Waniha ,HI
MIYAMOTO,Yasuo R.,442-I,Pahala ,HI
MIYAOKA,George S.,442-L,Honolulu ,HI
MIYASATO,Isami,100-D,Puuene ,HI
MIYATA,Tamotsu,100-D,Honolulu ,HI
MIYAZONO,Tokio,442-F,Honolulu ,HI
MIYOGA,Tsuyoshi,100-C,Lawai ,HI
MIYOKO,Noboru,100-B,Los Angeles ,CA
MIYOKO,Mitsuru E.,100-A,Salt Lake City ,UT
MIZOKAMI,Timothy I.,442-M,Berkley ,CA
MIZUKAMI,William S.,442-H,Auburn ,WA
MIZUMOTO,Larry T.,Savage 43-07,Honolulu ,HI

MIZUMOTO,Morio,100-F,Kapoho ,HI
MIZUTARI,Yukitaka T.,MIS,Honolulu ,HI
MOCHIZUKI,Henry T.,100-D,Honolulu ,HI
MORAN,Edward V.,100-B,
MORI,Kiyoto,100-D,Hanapepe ,HI
MORI,Shigeru,MIS,Murray ,UT
MORIGUCHI,Haluto,100-C,San Francisco ,CA
MORIGUCHI,Rokuro,100-A,HI
MORIHARA,Arthur Akira,100-A,Kealakekua ,HI
MORIHIRO,Roy T.,442-G,Cleveland ,OH
MORIKAWA,Haruto,442-E,Hilo ,HI
MORIKAWA,Hiromu,100-B,Kihei ,HI
MORIMOTO,Toshiaki,442-F,Hakalau ,HI
MORISAKI,Harold H.,100-A,Honolulu ,HI
MORISHIGE,,Joseph,100-B,Denver ,CO
MORISHITA,Takeo,442-L,Honolulu ,HI
MORITA,Iwao,100-F,Hanamaulu ,HI
MORIWAKI,George Kaoru,100-A,Waialua ,HI
MOSELEY,David Leander,442-I,
MOTOISHI,Hiroshi,100-D,Hakalau ,HI
MOTOKANE,Wilfred M.,MIS,Honolulu ,HI
MOTONAGA,Susumu,1399Eng,Honolulu ,HI
MOTOYAMA,Susumu,100-C,Honolulu ,HI
MUKAI,Hachiro,442-F,Morgan Hill ,CA
MUNEMORI,Sadao Spud,100-A,Glendale ,CA
MURAKAMI,Isami,442-E,Honolulu ,HI
MURAKAMI,Sakae,100-C,Honokaa ,HI
MURAKAMI,Tadataka,442-L,Kalopa ,HI
MURAKAMI,Toshio S.,100-A,Wailuku ,HI
MURAKAMI,Kiyoshi,442-G,Pocatello ,ID
MURAMOTO,Masaru,MIS,Honolulu ,HI
MURANAGA (MH),Kiyoshi K.,442-F,Los Angeles ,CA
MURASHIGE,Richard Kano,100-A,Lihue ,HI
MURATA,Robert Shigeru,442-L,Honolulu ,HI
MURONAKA,Larry H.,47thEng,Koloa ,HI
MURONAKA,Mitsugi,100-C,Papaikou ,HI
NAEMURA,Roy I.,100-B,Walla Walla ,WA
NAGAJI,Kazutomu Grover,100-B,Honolulu ,HI
NAGAMI,Hiroshi,442-F,Pepeekeo ,HI
NAGANO,Setsuo,100-A,Wainaku ,HI
NAGANO,Hiroshi F.,100-B,Pingree ,ID
NAGANO,Hiroshi F.,100-B,Pingree ,ID
NAGANUMA,Martin Mitsuyoshi,100-C,Lahaina ,HI
NAGAO,Goichi,100-C,Ninole ,HI

NAGAOKA,Hitoshi,100-D,Honolulu ,HI
NAGAOKA,Hitoshi,100-D,Honolulu ,HI
NAGATA,Jim,442-L,San Jose ,CA
NAGATA,Hideo,100-C,Paia ,HI
NAGATA,Taichi,442-E,Hilo ,HI
NAGATO,Fumitake,442-G,Brawley ,CA
NAITO,Kaoru,100-A,Lihue ,HI
NAJITA,Hitoshi,442-L,Haina ,HI
NAKAGAKI,Masaru,442-K,Woodland ,CA
NAKAGAWA,Usho,Army Unit,
NAKAGAWA,Hirao,100-B,Makaweli ,HI
NAKAHARA,Shoichi Stanley,Savage 43-07,Olaa ,HI
NAKAI,Hitoshi,100-B,Papaikou ,HI
NAKAMA,Masao R.,442-L,Peahi Haiku ,HI
NAKAMA,Shigenori,100-B,Waimea ,HI
NAKAMINE (MH),Shinyei,100-B,Waianae ,HI
NAKAMOTO,Seichi,442-G,Fresno. ,CA
NAKAMOTO,Joe K.,442-F,Lahaina ,HI
NAKAMURA,George I.,Savage 42-12,Watsonville ,CA
NAKAMURA,George S.,442-E,Al Campo ,CA
NAKAMURA,Ned Teiji,442-G,Gardena ,CA
NAKAMURA,Edward E.,100-D,Puuene ,HI
NAKAMURA,Henry Y.,100-C,Honolulu ,HI
NAKAMURA,Iwao,Hilo Induct,Kealakekua ,HI
NAKAMURA,Kosei,100-C,Hakalau ,HI
NAKAMURA,Tadao,442-F,Pahoa ,HI
NAKAMURA,Yoshimitsu,100-D,Hanalei ,HI
NAKAMURA,John M.,442-K,Marion Co ,IN
NAKAMURA,Masaki H.,Savage 43-07,Gold Bar ,WA
NAKAMURA (MH),William K.,442-G,Seattle ,WA
NAKANISHI,Masao,100-C,Halaula ,HI
NAKANO,Tsutomu,100-B,Makaweli ,HI
NAKASAKI,Robert K.,100-A,Los Angeles ,CA
NAKASHIMA,Raito R.,100-B,Pocatello ,ID
NAKASHIMA,Wataru,442-M,Pocatello ,ID
NAKATA,Alfred Y.,3rd Div,Portland ,OR
NAKAUYE,Donald T.,100-Hq,Honolulu ,HI
NAKAYA,Kiyoshi C.,168th-Inf,Sacramento ,CA
NAKAYAMA,Minoru,442-Can,Alameda ,CA
NAKAZATO,Saburo,100-B,Hakalau ,HI
NARIMATSU,John T.,442-L,Reedley ,CA
NEZU,Yutaka,100-B,Waimanalo ,HI
NII,Yoshito,Hilo Induct,Papaikou ,HI
NIIDE,Shigeto,442-G,Pepeekeo ,HI

NILGES Jr.,Edward J.,442-3Hq,
NINOMIYA,Takao T.,100-B,Fowler ,CA
NINOMIYA,Ban,442-E,Seattle ,WA
NISHI,Takanori A.,100-C,San Francisco ,CA
NISHI,Chikao,442-M,Papaikou ,HI
NISHIHARA,Kazuo,100-D,Puuene ,HI
NISHIKAWA,Akio,442Med,Paia ,HI
NISHIMOTO,Tom T.,442-L,El Centro ,CA
NISHIMOTO (MH),Joe M.,442-G,Fresno. ,CA
NISHIMURA,Shigeki,100-C,Honolulu ,HI
NISHIMURA,Wilfred K.,100-A,Honolulu ,HI
NISHISHITA,Charles J.,100-C,Honolulu ,HI
NISHITANI,Chieto,100-A,Kohala ,HI
NISHITANI,Taro,100-A,Honolulu ,HI
NITTA,Kongo,Army Unit,Watsonville ,CA
NODA,Sueo,100-B,Spreckelsville ,HI
NORITAKE,Yoshito,100-B,Seattle ,WA
NOZAKI,Albert Y.,100-B,Waialua ,HI
NOZAKI,Tadashi,442-G,Mokuleia ,HI
NOZAWA,Alfred S.,100-B,Honolulu ,HI
NUMA,Toshio,442-G,Kealia ,HI
OBA,Masayoshi,442-L,Lahaina ,HI
OBA,Sunichi G.,442-E,Lahaina ,HI
OBA,Stanley T.,442-G,Portland ,OR
OCHIAI,Larry M.,100-Md,Mountain View ,HI
OGATA,Fred S.,442-K,Paia ,HI
OGATA,Masaru,100-B,Honolulu ,HI
OGATA,Masayoshi,100-D,Hakalau ,HI
OGATA,Tsugio,100-B,Waimea ,HI
OGATA,Benjamin F.,442-K,TX
OGAWA,John N.,442-I,Garden Grove ,CA
OGAWA,Sadao,442-F,Eleele ,HI
OGAWA,Edward,100-C,Ashton ,ID
OGOMORI,Yoshio W.,100-A,Kekaha ,HI
OHAMA,Abraham G.,442-F,Sanger ,CA
OHKI,Arnold,442-K,Livingston ,CA
OISHI,Teiji T.,100-B,Hilo ,HI
OJIRI,Akira,100-F,Papaikou ,HI
OKADA,John T.,442-G,Palo Alto ,CA
OKAMOTO,James S.,442-K,San Francisco ,CA
OKAMOTO,Donald M.,100-B,Honolulu ,HI
OKAMOTO,James T.,442-K,Wainaku ,HI
OKAMOTO,Ralph S.,442-F,Honolulu ,HI
OKAMOTO,Tomiso,442-G,Wailuku ,HI

OKAZAKI,Isao,442-G,Seattle ,WA
OKAZAKI,Takaaki,442-L,Seattle ,WA
OKIDA,Katsunoshin,442-F,Los Angeles ,CA
OKIDO,Shoji,Hilo Induct,Honomu ,HI
OKIMOTO,Richard M.,100-A,Honolulu ,HI
OKU,Muneo L.,Hilo Induct,Koloa ,HI
OKUMA,Seiei,442-G,Kekaha ,HI
OKUMURA,Toyokazu,100-D,Pepeekeo ,HI
OKURA,Susumu,442-I,Wilmington ,CA
OLIVER,Harry E.,442-I,
OMOKAWA,George,442-G,San Pedro ,CA
OMURA,Ken,Savage 42-06,Seattle ,WA
ONAGA,Takeyasu T.,442-I,Spreckelsville ,HI
ONODERA,Satoru,100-C,Seattle ,WA
ONOYE,Lloyd M.,442-I,Salinas ,CA
OSATO,Reginald M.,Hilo Induct,Hilo,HI
OSHIRO,Choyei,442-I,Ulumalu ,HI
OSHIRO,Kenneth C.,100-D,Ewa ,HI
OSHIRO,Sam Y.,442-I,Paia ,HI
OSHIRO,Seikichi,442-G,Olaa ,HI
OSHIRO,Wallace H.,100-C,Papaikou ,HI
OSHIRO,Yeishin,100-B,Piihonua ,HI
OTA,Daniel C.,Savage 43-07,San Francisco ,CA
OTA,George,Army Unit,Parlier ,CA
OTA,Roy,100-C,Sacramento ,CA
OTA,Randall M.,100-D,Waipahu ,HI
OTAGURO,Tadashi,100-D,Honolulu ,HI
OTAKE,Masanao,100-C,Lahaina ,HI
OTANI,Douglas K.,100-C,Honolulu ,HI
OTANI (MH),Kazuo,442-G,Visalia ,CA
OTSUBO,Akira R.,442-L,Stockton ,CA
OTSUKA,Jiro,100-A,Anahola ,HI
OYABU,Harumatsu,442-L,Waiehu ,HI
OYAKAWA,Francis K.,442-E,Honolulu ,HI
OZAKI,Robert Y.,100-A,Honolulu ,HI
OZAWA,George Y.,100-A,Honolulu ,HI
PERRAS,Francis J.,100-A,
PETERSON,Roy T.,100-B,
POTTER JR,Ralph J.,442-M,Franklin Co ,IN
RAY,Neill M.,100-D,Marion Co ,TN
RIYU,Masatsugu,100-C,Wailuku ,HI
ROGERS,Ben W. Jr.,442-A.T,Little Rock ,AR
SADAYASU,Herbert K.,100-C,Honolulu ,HI
SAGAMI,Yohei,442-E,Fife ,WA

SAGIMORI,Tamemasa T.,442-L,Berkley ,CA

SAHARA,Atsuo,100-A,Honolulu ,HI

SAIKI,Masami,442-L,Lahaina ,HI

SAITO,Calvin T.,442-K,Los Angeles ,CA

SAITO,George S.,442-H,Los Angeles ,CA

SAITO,Chuji,100-D,Kapaa ,HI

SAITO,Kinji,100-Hq,Waipahu ,HI

SAITO,Tsukasa,MIS,Portland ,OR

SAKADO,Masuto,442-G,Laupahoehoe ,HI

SAKAI,Yoshinori,100-C,Sacramento ,CA

SAKAI,Richard M.,442-E,Aiea ,HI

SAKAMOTO,Atsushi,442-K,San Pedro ,CA

SAKAMOTO,Masami,442-E,Sacramento ,CA

SAKAMOTO,Louis K.,100-C,Waihee ,HI

SAKAMOTO,Noboru,442-I,Haw ,HI

SAKAMOTO,Robert I.,100-C,Hilo ,HI

SAKAMOTO,Uichi W.,100-A,Honaupo ,HI

SAKOHIRA,Todd T.,442-G,Fowler ,CA

SAMESHIMA,George S.,442-G,Salinas ,CA

SANMONJI,Uetaro W.,442-Hq,Hollywood ,CA

SASAKI,Yoshio F.,100-C,Kahaluu ,HI

SASANO,Toshio,100-A,Honolulu ,HI

SASAOKA,Itsumu,100-A,Aiea ,HI

SASE,Andrew Y,442-L,Gardena ,CA

SATO,Saburo,100-B,Waiakea Mill ,HI

SATO,Shukichi,100-F,Lawai ,HI

SATO,Takeo,442-I,Hilo ,HI

SATO,Shin,442-E,Beaverton ,OR

SATO,Tadao,442-Can,Seattle,WA

SATO,Yukio,442-I,Seattle ,WA

SAWADA,George K.,100-Md,Seattle ,WA

SCHEMEL,Kurt E.,100-E,NY

SEIKE,Toll,442-E,Seattle ,WA

SEKIMURA,Koichi K.,100-C,Hilo ,HI

SESHIKI,Hihumi,100-C,Hanamaulu ,HI

SHIBATA,Mitsuru,Savage 42-12,Fresno ,CA

SHIBATA,Kenneth K.,442-K,Haybro ,CO

SHIGAYA,Tetsuo,Army Unit,Mineral ,WA

SHIGEMURA,Masao F.,442-H,Seattle ,WA

SHIGETA,Hideo,100-A,Paia ,HI

SHIGEZANE,Masao,100-B,Los Angeles ,CA

SHIGIHARA,Takeshi,442-L,Puuene ,HI

SHIIGI,Shinichi,Hilo Induct,Honolulu ,HI

SHIKATA,George M.,MIS,Los Angeles ,CA

SHIKIYA,Ted T.,100-A,Honolulu ,HI

SHIMABUKU,Roy K.,100-A,Paia ,HI

SHIMABUKURO,Hideo,100-A,Honolulu ,HI

SHIMABUKURO,Tomoaki,442-2Hq,Waianae ,HI

SHIMADA,George M.,100-C,Greeley ,CO

SHIMATSU,Akira R.,442-3Hq,Los Angeles ,CA

SHIMIZU,Gordon S.,442-I,Aiea ,HI

SHIMIZU,Takeo,100-C,Hana ,HI

SHIMIZU,Jimmy T.,442-F,Seattle ,WA

SHINTANI,Takeo,442-E,Kahaluu ,HI

SHIOMICHI,Joe A.,442-I,Brawley ,CA

SHIOZAWA,Roy R.,100-A,Tyhee Jefferson Co ,ID

SHIRAKAWA,Raymond H.,Hilo

Induct,Waiohino ,HI

SHIRAMIZU,Kiyoshi J.,100-Md,Salinas ,CA

SHIROISHI,Shigeomi,MIS,

SHIROKANE,Kizo,100-C,Paia ,HI

SHIYAMA,Henry M.,100-C,Ookala ,HI

SHOJI,Toshiaki,442-E,Livingston ,CA

SOKEN,Yeishun,Hilo Induct,Waiakeauka ,HI

SUDA,David I.,100-C,Pauwela ,HI

SUEOKA,Sadamu R.,100-C,Prowers Co ,CO

SUEOKA,Theodore Teruo,100-C,Honolulu ,HI

SUGAHARA,Shinichi,442-L,Hanapepe ,HI

SUGAWARA,Senji S.,442-K,Waimea ,HI

SUGIYAMA,Hiroshi,442Hq/Md,San Francisco ,CA

SUGIYAMA,Togo S.,442-H,Los Angeles ,CA

SUGIYAMA,Itsuo,100-A,Kukuihaele ,HI

SUMIDA,Michiru,100-C,Marina ,CA

SUNADA,Albert M.,100-C,Kalihikai ,HI

SUWA,Nobuyuki,100-B,Lanai ,HI

SUYAMA,George W.,100-A,Harve ,MT

SUZAWA,Jiro,442-L,Kohala ,HI

SUZUKI,Takashi,100-E,Nawiliwili ,HI

SWEITZER,Edward H.,100-B,MD

TABATA,Teruo,100-B,Oakland ,CA

TABUCHI,Shigeo,442-I,Los Angeles ,CA

TAGAMI,Yoshio,442-F,Wahiawa ,HI

TAGUCHI,Hitoshi B.,100-D,Lahaina ,HI

TAHARA,Cooper T.,442-I,Sacramento ,CA

TAHIRA,George Y.,100-A,Kahaluu ,HI

TAIRA,Masaru,442-L,Honolulu ,HI

TAIRA,Seitoku,442-E,Hilo ,HI

TAKAGI,Boon E.,100-C,New York ,NY

TAKAGI,Boon E.,100-C,New York ,NY
TAKAHASHI,Arthur I.,442-I,Los Angeles ,CA
TAKAHASHI,Itsuo,100-D,Waipahu ,HI
TAKAHASHI,Manzo (Mon),442-I,Spokane ,WA
TAKAO,Thomas T.,100-C,San Francisco ,CA
TAKARA,Ronald K.,100-B,Onomea ,HI
TAKASAKI,Gordon K.,442-E,Kohala ,HI
TAKASUGI,Katsumi L.,100-C,Ventura ,CA
TAKATA,Shigeo Joe,100-B,Waialua ,HI
TAKAYAMA,John N.,442-L,Ookala ,HI
TAKAYAMA,Yoshito J.,442-K,Ookala ,HI
TAKEBA,Masaharu,100-B,Honolulu ,HI
TAKEDA,Jim,Army Unit,
TAKEHARA,Shoichi J.,100-C,Fife ,WA
TAKEI,Yoshinobu,100-A,Puuene ,HI
TAKEMOTO,Haruo,442-L,Wahiawa ,HI
TAKEMOTO,Iwao,442-K,Kapaa ,HI
TAKEMOTO,Tom (Tami),442-K,Clatskine ,OR
TAKEMURA,Isao S.,Army Unit,Hilo ,HI
TAKENAKA,Tooru,442-E,Hanalei ,HI
TAKEO,Robert M.,100-C,Kaunakakai ,HI
TAKETA,Shigeto,442-I,Papaikou ,HI
TAKETA,William H.,100-C,Kent ,WA
TAKETA,Jimmy Y.,442-K,WA
TAKEUCHI,Ichiro S.,Army Unit,Oakland ,CA
TAKEUCHI,Tadashi,100-B,Sacramento ,CA
TAKUBO,Kenji,442-K,Honolulu ,HI
TAMANAHA,Douglas Kunio,442Med,Kahuluu ,HI
TAMANAHA,Masao H.,442-K,Peahi Haiku,HI
TAMASHIRO,Thomas T.,442-I,Koloa ,HI
TAMURA,Toyoshi,100-A,Honolulu ,HI
TAMURA,Masaru R.,442-F,Fife ,WA
TANAHASHI,Kei,442-G,Los Angeles ,CA
TANAKA,Seiji,442-M,
TANAKA,John Y.,100-C,Los Angeles ,CA
TANAKA,K.O.,442-K,Lodi ,CA
TANAKA,Jack Manabu,100-B,Pahala ,HI
TANAKA,Jiro,442-L,Makaweli ,HI
TANAKA,Keichi,100-B,Waimanalo ,HI
TANAKA,Harley,442-M,Mitchell ,NE
TANAKA,Matsusaburo,100-C,Seattle ,WA
TANAMACHI,Saburo,442-E,San Benito ,TX
TANI,Bushichi,Hilo Induct,Papaikou ,HI
TANIMOTO,Larry T.,442-I,Honomu ,HI

TANIMOTO,Teruto,100-C,Paia ,HI
TANIMOTO,Yukio E.,442-E,Honomu ,HI
TANJI,Mitsuo,442-F,Waialua ,HI
TANOUYE,Ted T.,442-K,Torrance ,CA
TANOUYE,Katsushi,100-D,Kurtistown ,HI
TASHIMA,Masaru,442-I,Fresno. ,CA
TATEYAMA,Haruyoshi,100-F,Kailua ,HI
TATSUMI,George,442-E,Seattle ,WA
TENGAN,Masaru,442-L,Koloa ,HI
TENGWAN,Yoshio,100-C,Lahaina ,HI
TERADA,Henry M.,100-B,Honolulu ,HI
TERAMAE,Ted A.,442-H,Onomea ,HI
TERAMOTO,Lloyd M.,100-B,Waianae ,HI
TERAMOTO,Shizuo,100-B,Pepeekeo ,HI
TERUYA,Herman T.,100-D,Ninole ,HI
TERUYA,Kenkichi K.,100-D,Waikapu ,HI
TERUYA,Kenkichi Kenneth,100-D,Waikapu ,HI
TESHIMA,Michio,100-C,Riverside ,CA
TESHIMA,Robert T.,Army Unit,New Providence ,NJ
TEZUKA,Theodore T.,100-A,Los Angeles ,CA
TOGO,Shiro,100-A,Kahaluu ,HI
TOKUNAGA,Clifford T.,442-F,Honolulu ,HI
TOKUSATO,Hidetoshi,442-L,Waiakeauka ,HI
TOKUSHIMA,Harry H.,442-I,Los Angeles ,CA
TOKUSHIMA,Patrick M.,100-B,Honolulu ,HI
TOKUYAMA,Minoru,100-Md,Honolulu ,HI
TOMA,Tsugiyasu,442-G,Hilo ,HI
TOMA,Yasukichi J.,100-A,Hakalau ,HI
TOMIKAWA,Calvin T.,442-E,Honolulu ,HI
TOMITA,Hiroichi,442-F,Wailuku ,HI
TOMITA,Isami,100-C,Paia ,HI
TOMITA,Nobuaki,522-A,Honolulu ,HI
TONAI,Taro,100-C,Waikapu ,HI
TOSAKA,Minoru,100-D,Haiku ,HI
TOYAMA,Richard K.,100-A,Hamakua ,HI
TOYAMA,Shinsuke,442-L,Puuene ,HI
TOYOTA,Shichizo,442-E,Gilroy ,CA
TSUKAMOTO,Daniel Y.,100-D,Los Angeles ,CA
TSUKANO,Ichiro,100-D,Pepeekeo ,HI
TSUMAKI,Kenichi,442-K,Idaho Falls ,ID
TSUNEMATSU,Bertram A,442-K,Los Angeles Co ,CA
TSUNO,Isao J.,MIS,Alvarado ,CA
TSUTSUI,Kazumi,100-D,Pahoa ,HI
UCHIMA,Yasuji M.,100-A,Kukuihaele ,HI

UEJO,James K.,100-D,Kalaheo ,HI
UEMOTO,Kazumi,100-A,Waiakea Mill ,HI
URABE,Howard M.,442-G,Kapaa ,HI
UYEDA,Moriichi,100-E,Wahiawa ,HI
UYENO,Theodore T.,232Eng,Honolulu ,HI
WADA,Daniel M.,100-B,Anahola ,HI
WAKITA,Masuo,Army Unit,Kern Co ,CA
WASADA,Kenneth Y.,100-E,Honolulu ,HI
WASANO,Shigeo,442-2Hq,Paia-Maui ,HI
WATANABE,Hiroshi,442-L,Honolulu ,HI
WATANABE,Kiyotoshi,442-3Hq,Lahaina ,HI
WATANABE,Theodore H.,442-I,Pullman ,WA
WHEATLEY,James David,442-I,Demopolis ,AL
WHITE JR,Floyd Earl,442-G,
YAGI,Steve Seiko,442-G,Lahaina ,HI
YAMADA,Hideo,442-F,Kihei ,HI
YAMADA,Raymond T.,442-3Hq,Honolulu ,HI
YAMAGUCHI,Robert M.,1525Eng,Waialua ,HI
Yamaguchi,George T.,Savage 43-07,Portland ,OR
YAMAJI,Iwao Bill,143rd-Inf,Mountain View ,CA
YAMAMIZU,Torao,Hilo Induct,Pepeekeo ,HI
YAMAMOTO,Fred M.,442-K,Palo Alto ,CA
YAMAMOTO,John Hiroshi,442-H,Sanger ,CA
YAMAMOTO,John Tsuyoshi,442-H,Oceanside ,CA
YAMAMOTO,George I.,442Hq/Md,Honolulu ,HI
YAMAMOTO,Masaru,100-A,Waialua ,HI
YAMAMOTO,Takeo,232Eng,Aiea ,Hi
YAMANAGA,Thomas Isamu,100-A,Honolulu ,HI
YAMAOKA,Tsutomu,442-F,Hamakua ,HI
YAMASAKI,Harry Shizuo,442-I,Honolulu ,HI
YAMASHIRO,Gordon Kenshi,442-K,Kapaa ,HI
YAMASHIRO,Lei Seijiro,100-C,Lahaina ,HI
YAMASHITA,Kazuo,100-D,Waimea ,HI
YAMASHITA,Setsuro,442-F,Seattle ,WA
YAMAUCHI,Chiyoaki Jerry,442-I,Wahiawa ,HI
YAMAURA,Gordon G.,442-K,Seattle ,WA
YANO,Albert H.,Hilo Induct,Koloa ,HI
YASUDA,Fred S.,442-K,Los Angeles ,CA
YASUDA,Joe R.,100-C,Santa Rosa ,CA
YASUHIRA,Arata,442-M,Wailuku ,HI
YASUI,Yoji O.,100-C,Wailuku ,HI
YASUI,Hideo,442-E,Olympia ,WA
YETO,Mitsuru T.,442-L,Oxnard ,HI
YOGI,Matsuichi,442-K,Waipahu ,HI

YONAMINE,Hideo,442-F,Lahaina ,HI
YONEKURA,Satoshi,7.390-MP,Hayward ,CA
YONEMURA,Hitoshi,442-Can,Los Angeles ,CA
YONEMURA,Yonezo,Hilo Induct,Keopu Kona ,HI
YOSHIDA,Minoru M.,442-E,Linden ,CA
YOSHIDA,Kenjiro,442-L,St. Petersburg ,FL
YOSHIDA,Edward Yoshiharu,100-C,Naalehu ,HI
YOSHIGAI,Mitsuichi,442-H,Wailuku ,HI
YOSHIHARA,Makoto,Army Unit,Guadalupe ,CA
YOSHIHARA,Toraichi,442-E,Kapaa ,HI
YOSHIMURA,Jacob Yoshio,442-G,Hilo ,HI
YOSHIMURA,Minoru,100-A,Honolulu ,HI
YOSHIMURA,Saburo,442-L,Pearl City ,HI
YOSHINAGA,Akira,442-G,Los Angeles ,CA
YOSHIOKA,Isami,442-L,Hilo ,HI
YOSHIOKA,Shigeo,Army Unit,Seattle ,WA
YOSHIZAKI,Tatsuo,100-C,Norwalk ,CA
YUNOKI,Shiyoji,442-K,Boulder,CO

Photograph / Image Credits

Page 5: Map courtesy of History Department, United States Military Academy (USMA)

Page 10: National Archives and Records Administration (NARA), College Park, MD (Ohata)

Page 11: NARA, (Hayashi)

Page 11: NARA, (Hasemoto)

Page 13: The Bancroft Library. University of California, Berkeley. Used by permission.

Page 14: The Bancroft Library. University of California, Berkeley. Used by permission.

Page 14: NARA, College Park, MD

Page 18: NARA, College Park, MD SC-176302

Page 18: NARA, College Park, MD SC-180026

Page 19: NARA, College Park, MD SC-180029

Page 21: University of Utah, Marriott Library, Used by permission

Page 24: History Department, United States Military Academy (USMA)

Page 25: Rivista Aeronautica (Italian Air Force Magazine)

Page 32: History Department, USMA,

Page 36: NARA, (Davila)

Page 37: NARA, (Kobashigawa)

Page 39: NARA, (Nakamine)

Page 42: NARA, (Muranaga)

Page 45: History Department, USMA

Page 46: NARA, (Nakamura)

Page 46: NARA, (Ono)

Page 47: NARA, College Park, MD SC-340435

Page 49: NARA, College Park, MD SC-340930

Page 49: NARA, College Park, MD SC-340924

Page 51: NARA, (Motto)

Page 52: NARA, College Park, MD SC-340918

Page 52: NARA, College Park, MD SC-192068

Page 53: NARA, (Otani)

Page 54: NARA, (Nakae)

Page 54: NARA, College Park, MD SC-340923

Page 55: NARA, College Park, MD SC-340925

Page 57: History Department, USMA,

Page 59: NARA, College Park, MD SC-195140

Page 59: NARA, College Park, MD SC-340944

Page 61: (Ohama) California State University, Sacramento Library, Used by permission.

Page 63: NARA, (Kuroda)

Page 65: NARA, College Park, MD SC-340943

Page 67: NARA, (Hajiro)

Page 74: NARA, (Dahlquist)

Page 75: NARA, College Park, MD SC-253983

Page 78: NARA, College Park, MD SC-195903

Page 80: NARA, (Okubo)

Page 84: NARA, (Sakato)

Page 86: NARA, College Park, MD SC-340928

Page 90: U.S. Army Art Collection

Page 94: NARA, College Park, MD SC-341438

Page 93: NARA, (Nichimoto)

Page 96: NARA, College Park, MD SC-196716

Page 106: History Department, USMA

Page 108: NARA, (Munemori)

Page 105: NARA, College Park, MD SC-340934

Page 111: NARA, College Park, MD SC-205288

Page 114: NARA, (Okutsu)

Page 116: NARA, College Park, MD SC-205356

Page 118: NARA, (Inouye)

Page 121: NARA, (Hayashi)

Page 127: Go For Broke Foundation, used by permission

Page 129: NARA, College Park, MD 127-GW-325-110958

Page 131: NARA, College Park, MD SC-122933

Page 134: NARA, (Calugas)

Page 135: NARA, (Wai)

Page 139: NARA, College Park, MD SC-212046

Page 141: NARA, S College Park, MD C-250635

Pages 146-168: NARA

Index

9 780979 689611